Missional Body

the beauty and purpose of the church

by michael
griffiths

Copyright © 2019 Bold Grace Ministries

410 N Bonham Dr.
Allen, TX 75013
www.boldgrace.org

Library of Congress Cataloging in Publication Data

Griffiths, Michael (1928-)
Missional Body: The Beauty and Purpose of the Church

1. Church. 2. Missions I. Title

ISBN: **978-0-9994374-1-4**

Cover Design: Bold Grace Ministries
Prepared for print by: Mary A. Cooper and Jeremy D. Edmondson
Edited for publication by: Jeremy D. Edmondson
Typesetting: Holly Melton

Printed in the United States of America

Table of Contents

Preface to the New Edition VII

Editor's Preface XI

Introduction XV

Chapter 1 - Our Mental Concept of the Church . . 1

Chapter 2 - Salvation More Than Personal 11

Chapter 3 - Salvation Under Construction. 23

Chapter 4 - Salvation Corporate and
Co-Operative. 35

Chapter 5 - The Goal of Salvation. 51

Chapter 6 - The Church as a Family Community 63

Chapter 7 - The Church and the Student. 79

Chapter 8 - The Church and its Services 97

Chapter 9 - The Church and Missions. 109

Chapter 10 - The Church Militant. 125

About Bold Grace Ministries 151

Preface to the New Edition

Is it possible to be disappointed that the demand for one's book after more than 40 years justifies a new edition? As affirming as this might be to this reflective 90 year old, I do confess to a slight sense of disappointment. How wonderful might it have been to say that *'the ragged Cinderella, hideous among the ashes'* had advanced in her understanding of her corporate identity and call in this time? Yet four decades on I regret that this book appears to be as relevant as ever.

In my concluding chapter I quote the former Prime Minister of Singapore Lee Kwan Yew; *"Change is the essence of life"*. And there's no doubt things have changed enormously not least in my own church life in the intervening years. Since 1975 I have been thrilled to see the establishment of Japanese Christian Fellowship (JCF) as a thriving ex-patriate community in Singapore. At the beginning of the 80s, I returned to my home country of the UK to become principal of London Bible College (now London School of Theology) and enjoyed ten years in fellowship with Northwood Hills Evangelical Church in the outskirts of London. I then spent my remaining working years as Head of Mission studies at Regent College Vancouver and membership of the church there. The 1990s saw me retiring back to Guildford, UK and worshipping once again at Millmead Baptist Church - featured in this book – where I continue to worship today.

But what of change in the Church worldwide? In certain ways – praise God – there has been much positive change. I am delighted that Chapter 9 needs to be reread through the lens of much blessing and growth. The strength of newly planted churches in the two thirds world is cause for heartfelt rejoicing. The globalisation of mission which, in the 1970's was still in a pioneering phase in many parts of the world has seen a substantial shift from predominantly colonial models towards true global evangelisation with so-called mission fields from the 1970s now becoming significant sending nations. Additionally, the increasing mobility of migrant communities has seen new opportunities for Christians called to evangelise their compatriots in far flung diaspora populations. Again, praise be to God.

But there has been much change which should give the church cause for concern. In the western world we have seen declining church attendance and membership and an increase in second and third generations of so-called 'unchurched' families. Gone are the days when one might assume some prior knowledge of the gospel, however small, when witnessing to a friend or neighbour. Certainly in 'post-Christendom' UK we are coming to terms with the fact that the majority of the population have little idea of what happens in our churches, necessitating a return towards a 'zero assumptions' pioneering approach to evangelism.

In terms of cultural mindset the surge in post-modern values such as relativism and individualism has had huge repercussions on world views with knock-on implications for our preaching and teaching. In the original edition I allude to a tendency to overstate the personal at the expense of the communal and to emphasise private religious experience over corporate. How much greater the challenge now in an increasingly individualistic world. And likewise, how great the challenge of preaching the objective truth of Christ in a 'post-truth' society which holds that every individual's perception of 'truth' is legitimate.

In Chapter 6 I note; *"many of us already find our programmes are over-extended"* and question whether couples and young families have sufficient time to participate in church life. Since then, in most parts of the world, there has been a marked increase in working hours which, coupled with increasing numbers of dual-income households places huge strains on family time, particularly at the weekend. This naturally compromises the participation in body life and, in many churches, leads to much of the mid-week voluntary work shifting to the older generation.

The world is much changed indeed, leading me somewhat paradoxically, to the sobering conclusion that in terms of calling the Church to arms, nothing has changed. As I originally noted, *"This book is pressing the importance of the doctrine of the church upon a generation which has neglected and undervalued it…"* I would echo this all the more today, adding that secular and societal trends have, if anything, added to the challenge.

But, as I have said before, I will say again; we should not be down-hearted. I stand by my sentiment in Chapter 10 that we must all have absolute assurance that the gates of hell will not prevail against the Church. Cinderella may still need guiding in her purpose but she is far from conquered. One is reminded of that sage quote: "*The church is a perpetually defeated thing which far outlives her conquerors.*" I give thanks for the resilience of Christ's beautiful Bride through the centuries and I continue to have confidence in the restoring power of God and share Paul's vision that the Almighty's 'victorious counterculture' is on the march.

I conclude, as I did all those years ago: "*Better start praying then about how to realise it.*"

Yours ever in Christ

Dr Mike Griffiths

Editor's Preface

The Church is beautiful. This is how God sees it. Yet, we would be quick to add in our minds that our daily experience with the Church routinely disappoints us despite its divine assessment. Something inside of us cries out, "This should not be so!" And why? Because we are deeply convinced that the Church is God's only present-day entity commissioned for making disciples of the world. We are convinced of this because this is what the Scriptures clearly convey. Only the Church has been put forward as the light-bearers of God's unchanging truth. And because the Church is "in Christ," its identity has already been established in extolling the Lord Jesus Christ as the Savior of the world, but also as the prime target for the enemy of God. The supernaturally embedded hopes that come with being in Christ can quickly rise up within us and we become expectant of the Church to lay hold of its divine potential. We know that the Church was commissioned to do not just great things, but God-things, having His Truth, indwelt with His Spirit, being bought by His blood, having His righteousness, and being given the unimaginable potential, as those who are in Christ, to be found holy and blameless before Him in our love for one another! The Scriptures preach to us of the divine realities that have been graciously lavished upon us in Christ and our hearts sing, our cups overflow, and our joy for what God can do through the Body of Christ is once again blazing anew. We then quickly divebomb back into reality when we look upon a Body of believers who seem largely disjointed, devoid of intimate fellowship, shackled with division and factions, substituting Christ's Bride with subset organizations, with barely a scent of God's Word hanging in the air.

In 1975, Michael Griffiths recognized these inconsistencies and had concluded that the Church of God had experienced an identity crisis. His analysis identified an individuality, and even a narcissism, that had overtaken the *koinōnia* that was to sanctify the Church from society. The mindset of those in Christ was about seeking to progress for the sake of self, rather than claiming the unity, the "joined-together," the "built-together," the "body-together" that the Church should be. The Church as a whole was not being true to herself as God had carefully and intentionally designed her. The Church was failing to see that meeting with one another for prayer, quality time in the Word of God, and the corporate singing and praising of our mighty God is the very display of what it means to be His *ekklēsia*.

Upon reading the 1975 edition, I could not help but to feel that Griffiths had written everything that I had been feeling or had ever wanted to say about the current state of the Church. Though I am living in the 21st Century, Griffiths' words carried relevance to Christianity's current dilemmas, despite being more than 40 years removed. Every page bypassed the symptoms that clergy often waste their time treating and placed its finger on the direct nerve that was fueling our current problems. Griffiths understood that the key to turning the Church back to its God-prescribed glory and beauty lay in the re-education of God's Word to the people of God with an emphasis on the glorious position and calling that the Church had been given and taking the necessary steps to see that truth as a daily experience. The inward focus of the local congregation must be laid to rest and the city, state, nation, and global calling of missions must be embraced. Even in his time, Griffiths understood that to be a radically different church was to simply be a biblical church that lived out these truths because many others had capitulated away from the Scriptures. Congregations must engage and be intimately available to one another, not just in their local context, but in their connections across the world. We are not isolationists, but should be conversationalists because we actually have something to say; and we have something worth hearing.

Thus, the reprinting of this unknown classic was a must. The shelves at the local Christian bookstore will have nothing of this caliber on them. This book needed to be reprinted to fill a void that is only getting worse as time goes on. My repeated prayer for the publication of this work is that it will drive the reader back to the Scriptures, and by embracing all that the Scriptures have to say about the Church, intentional change will take place in his or her local congregation. May our churches become unified, vibrant, gracious, loving, missional, and obedient as we stay the course in promoting the eternal life that Christ freely offers the world!

Getting this work ready for republication was a blessing. Aiding greatly in this endeavor was Mary Cooper, who served in typing out half of this work, proof-reading the new manuscript, and offering editorial suggestions along the way. The translation that is largely used has been changed from the Revised Standard Version to the English Standard Version. Any references to the text in exact form have been largely maintained for the sake of letting the author be true to his own thoughts.

Jeremy Edmondson

September 2018

Introduction

Christians collectively seem to be suffering from a strange amnesia. A high proportion of people who "go to church" have forgotten what it is all for. Week by week they attend services in a special building and go through their particular, time-honored routine, but give little thought to the purpose of what they are doing.

The Bible talks about "the bride of Christ," but the church today seems like a ragged Cinderella, hideous among the ashes. She has forgotten that she is supposed to be growing up, as the soap advertisements used to have it, "to be a beautiful lady!" Many Christians can rattle off glibly the various biblical pictures of the church as "building," and "body," and "bride"; but in their experience these ideas have never got beyond a theoretical stage, and they continue to be disappointed with, and disillusioned by, the church as they know it. I have often noticed when serving on question panels that many of the apparently *individual* problems of Christians stem from the inadequacy of their *congregational* involvement, and their consequent dissatisfaction with the church.

The aim of this book is to restate the biblical doctrine of the church in contemporary terms and to relate it to our daily living as members of an ordinary local congregation of Christians.

Missional Body: The Beauty and Purpose of the Church is the logical successor to the books I was earlier asked to write. *Take My Life*—but for what purpose? The answer is simply, "To build a glorious new community!" Or again, I recently asked a young Filipino holding a copy of *Give Up Your Small Ambitions* what larger ambition took their place, and was delighted when he replied, "To build the church." *Consistent Christianity* attempted to deal with our behavior as Christian individuals; this book aims to apply the same biblical principles to our corporate behavior as Christian congregations. It has been written in the midst of a busy life, preoccupied with the missionary task and with little time for quiet thinking. Yet, all the time I have been thankfully conscious that the Lord has been leading and shaping my thinking through the things he has allowed to happen, through the mutual stimulation of conversation with fellow believers, through many helpful books, through preparing Bible readings on Ephesians and Colossians and, perhaps most of all, through congregations of which we have been privileged to be members—notably the Koganei Church in Tokyo and the Millmead Baptist Church in Guildford.

The theme relates directly, of course, to my involvement as a missionary in Asia. What, after all, is the aim of all missionary work, and indeed all Christian work properly conceived? It is not merely to harvest the unharvested field, but also to build the uncompleted building. We are seeking to start new congregations here in Asia which will be colonies of heaven on earth, wonderful new communities among whom God dwells. We are as concerned about corporate sanctification as we are about individual sanctification—not only with the perfecting of individual Christian men and women, but with the perfecting of Christian congregations all over the world.

We are as much concerned about a "new society" as any revolutionary New Leftist or neo-Arcadian. But for us this new and glorious society is the church of God. We do not anticipate establishing the kingdom of God on earth. For we recognize that the church down here is in a mere "caterpillar" stage. Yet it is none the less very much a kingdom-in-preparation, the new community in embryo. Sadly, many Christians seem to have lost their way corporately and are suffering from this strange amnesia about their congregational goals and purpose. This disregard of a major biblical doctrine is not confined to those concerned merely with the performance of rituals at regular intervals in buildings specially set apart for that purpose. The doctrine of the church may equally be disregarded by evangelists who evangelize for evangelism's sake, and who apparently see the church merely as an incidental and not particularly effective means of grace to help individuals get to heaven.

The younger generation is alienated by the hideous disfigurement, the repulsive "spots" and "wrinkles" of the institutional church, and is so disturbed and disenchanted that the church becomes an embarrassment to be explained away and replaced by new forms. As a result, there is currently a noticeable retreat from corporate responsibility into a subjective stress on private experience, and an enthusiasm for participation in group activity right outside the organized churches.

It is my conviction that a fresh understanding of the biblical doctrine of the church practically related to our daily, corporate activities as Christians, can and will give a new sense of purpose and direction to our Christian lives. The church is not a third class waiting room where we twiddle our thumbs while we wait for first class accommodation in heaven. It is a dynamic new community, winsome and attractive, and with an eternal significance in the purpose of God. The Bible makes it clear that the church is God's goal for mankind, for the new humanity in its new communities.

 God planned the church. Christ gave himself for the church. The Spirit is building us together in the church. I hope that this book will make us concerned, ready to give our lives for the building of God's church.

If there were a dedication to this book it would be to the late Reverend Alan Stibbs from whose teaching I profited so much as a schoolboy and as a student, and whose speaking and writing about the doctrine of the church especially has been formative in my own thinking.

M. C. Griffiths
Singapore, 1974

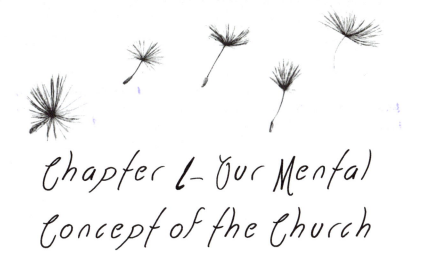

Chapter 1 – Our Mental Concept of the Church

… the church, which is His body,… (Eph 1:22b-23a)

When we begin thinking about the church our greatest difficulty is not its definition, although that in itself is far from simple. The big problem is sorting out the kind of picture conjured up in our minds by the words we use. What mental concept do we have when we think about Christians corporately, whether we call it church, chapel, assembly, kirk, or anything else? For example, how can we know what words to use when translating from the biblical Hebrew or Greek into any other language terms such as *theos* (God) or *ekklēsia* (church)? It is rarely possible to find exact equivalents.

Normally, of course, translators have to use some existing word that people already know and use and which conveys some meaning to the hearers. But this faces us with a very real dilemma. Its associations and origins may be entirely different, and it will need redefining in its new Christian sense. Inevitably, therefore, there is a danger of distorting the biblical meaning. In some languages it is possible to create a compound word which, although new, will still convey some kind of meaning to those who hear it. Languages such as Chinese which use ideographs lend themselves to this. Alternatively, the translator can use a foreign word and inject into it the meaning he wants.

When Tyndale translated the Bible into English he translated the word *ekklēsia* as "congregation" throughout, avoiding the use of the word "church" except in Acts 19:37, which he translated as "robbers of heathen churches," a reading retained by the Authorized (King James) Version but replaced in the Revised Version by "robbers of temples." British and American church history might have been quite different had Tyndale's translation been sustained.

Unfortunately, the translators of the AV used the word "church" where Tyndale had used the word "congregation." Both the English word "church" and the Scottish equivalent "kirk" appear to have been derived from the Greek adjective *kyriakos* meaning "the Lord's house."[1] In English this word "church" now has a very wide area of meaning and can be used for a building, a congregation, a denomination (as in "Council of Churches"), for the ministers and hierarchy of the "established" church and of course for the whole universal church of Christ. There seems little doubt that the building-centered concept of the church held by the ordinary British man in the street is the unfortunate legacy of this badly solved problem of Bible translation. To the average Briton the "church" is either the building down the road or an outdated institution.

Several European languages derive their word direct from *ekklēsia*, so that we find *église* (French) and *eglwys* (Welsh). Even in Asia we find derivations through European languages in *egregia* (Philippines) and *geredja* (Indonesia). In German there is the useful distinction between *Kirche* (also derived from *kyriakos*) and the *Gemeinde*; which Luther seems to have used of the true church of real believers.

In Japan, Korea, and China, altogether the pronunciation differs as *kyo-okai* (Japanese), *kyoohei* (Korean) and *jahwei* (Mandarin) the same pair of Chinese characters is used, expressing in all three languages the idea of "teaching association." This accommodates perfectly to Confucian ideas indigenous to these cultures. Unfortunately, however, it suggests that the church is an intellectual circle, an adult educational group being lectured in the classroom by the professional religious teacher. It tends to produce a class of lay spectators and listeners and has almost certainly hindered church growth and a true understanding of the church.

Can you see the problem now? These illustrations show that the word we use inevitably affects the way we think, and our view of the church is colored accordingly. We have the option either of trying to coin an entirely new word free of confusing associations and giving it the full biblical content, or of continuing to use what has become the traditional word "church," and endeavoring to reshape our own mental concepts so that we think correctly and biblically when we use the word.

---

[1] See D.W.B. Robinson's article, "Church," in *The New Bible Dictionary* (Grand Rapids: Eerdmans, 1962), p. 228.

The Meaning of the Word *Ekklēsia*

In the ordinary secular Greek of the first century AD this was the very ordinary word for a meeting. It can be used for any regular gathering; for example, the political gathering of a community meeting to make decisions, rather like those which continue in some of the Swiss cantons to this day. It was the word used for the large gathering in the theatre at Ephesus which was dismissed by the town clerk (Acts 19:32, 41, translated "assembly"). It was also used for the various spontaneous associations in Greek society that were always *religious* societies in that they gave formal expression to their unity in the worship of a god. For example, the silversmiths at Ephesus would have a guild which worshipped Diana. The term "*ekklēsia* of God," used by Christians, identified their "society" as a religious association of the type familiar to all. It was nothing unusual, just another of the many unofficial associations.[2] But although Christians were using an everyday word, they were using it, as the qualification shows, with a specific and limited meaning to describe themselves corporately as the assembly of God, or the church of Christ. The fact that it is God's group rather than ours has far reaching implications, as we shall see.

To understand this word fully, we must also remember that it was already familiar to readers of the Greek version of the Old Testament, the Septuagint, which was the "Common Bible" both of the Jews and of the first-century church. It was used to describe the "congregation" or "assembly" of Israel, especially where they were summoned together to meet the Lord (Deut 4:10; 9:10; 18:16; 31:30; Judg 20:2). Stephen used the word when he spoke of "the congregation in the wilderness" (Acts 7:38). We also meet this usage in Hebrews 2:12, quoting from Psalm 22:22.

Christian usage of the word "church" often suggests something static and inactive, a passive congregation sitting, docile, in their pews. This Old Testament background gives it a different flavor. The "church in the wilderness" was something dynamic, a people on the move, migrating together to a glorious destination. They had been brought traumatically out of Egypt, summoned to Sinai to meet the Lord, and called to go with him through the wilderness to the promised land. We shall find strong echoes of this much more purposeful view of the church in the New Testament. As Lesslie Newbigin says, "The church is the pilgrim people of God. It is on the move—hastening to the ends of the earth to beseech

---

[2] See E.A. Judge, *The Social Patterns of Christian Groups in the First Century* (London: Tyndale Press, 1960), pp. 40ff.

all men to be reconciled to God, hastening to the end of time to meet its Lord who will gather all into one."[3]

The 'Summoned Out' Group

A congregation does not just chance to come together; for the *ekklēsia* is specifically summoned together by God. The Greek derivation of the word is very closely related to the verb "to call" (*kaleō*) and the noun "calling" (*klēsis*). This relationship is obvious in Greek but often obscured in English. For example, the great prayer finishing, "To him be glory in the church and in Christ Jesus" (Eph 3:21a), does not at first sight seem to lead on to the words, artificially cut off from it by the introduction of a new chapter heading (Paul did not put chapter and verse headings in his Letters!), "I therefore… urge you to walk in a manner worthy of the calling to which you have been called," (Eph 4:1). God is to be glorified in the church. But how? By Christians walking worthy of the calling whereby they have been called. The force of it can be grasped by reading, "Walk worthy of the churching whereby you have been churched!" The relationship of "call," "calling," and "church" in Greek is as obvious as that between "prove," "approval," and "approbation" in English.

This word group and its Hebrew equivalent occur more than 700 times in the Old and New Testaments. It means not only to call someone by name, but more commonly to summon someone, to invite them and call them to come. In the garden of Eden, the Lord God called to Adam. Later he called, "Samuel! Samuel!" (Gen 3:9; 1 Sam 3:4a, RSV). The concept is a rich one and it is worth noticing several aspects of God's summoning of the congregation of Israel.

First, they were *called out*; it was a *deliverance*. We see this in Abraham's being called out of the city of Ur, as well as in the Israelites' being called out of Egypt and later out of Babylon. For Christians the call means deliverance out of sin and death.

Second, they were *called for* a relationship with God. This idea is expressed as a *covenant* between man and God (e.g. in God's dealings with Abraham and Moses). So Christians are "called into the fellowship of his Son" (1 Cor 1:9b), which refers not only to our future destination but also to our present relationship with him.

---

[3] Lesslie Newbigin, *The Household of God* (New York: Friendship Press, 1953), p. 25.

Third, they were *called* to a future *inheritance*. For them it was the promised land of Canaan: for Christians it is heaven. The idea of travelling to a destination is common in the Bible. We "share in a heavenly calling" (Heb 3:1b). Paul speaks of the "upward call" (Phil 3:14b), and encourages Timothy to "take hold of the eternal life to which you were called" (1 Tim 6:12b).

Fourth, they were *called together* to be a special *people* for God's own possession (Deut 7:6). Abraham, when he was called, was promised descendants like the sand and stars in number. Moses was promised that God would make a great nation out of those he was leading from Egypt. We see, therefore, that the summons of God is not just something personal and individual; it calls together a congregation, the "people of God." All this rich depth of meaning is found in this word *ekklēsia*.

The Scope of the *Ekklēsia*

Within the New Testament, *ekklēsia* is used to describe two main concepts. First, we have the idea of the *universal church*; that is, the total, worldwide Christian community made up of all Christians living and dead—"one Catholick and Apostolick Church" as the Nicene Creed has it. This seems to be the usage in Ephesians and Colossians (Eph 1:22; 3:10, 21; Col 1:18, 24).

Secondly, however, the word is often used to describe that same community in *local circumscription*.[4] As Newbigin expressed it, "'Congregation of God' is equally the proper title for a small group meeting in a house, and for the whole worldwide family. This is because the real character of it is determined by the fact that God is gathering it."[5]

The late Alan Stibbs had an apt illustration of this double use in which he would point out that we use the one expression "the moon" whether we are viewing the full moon, the half-moon or even the slenderest of crescent moons. Even though we see only a small section of it, we still remark, "Look at the moon!" In fact, in any case, we see only one side of the moon from earth it is impossible to see it all at once. In the same way,

---

[4] A useful phrase taken from G. Kittel, *A Theological Dictionary of the New Testament*, III (Grand Rapids: Eerdmans, 1968), p. 503.

[5] Newbigin, *Household*, p. 28.

we never see the whole of the church; yet, even when we see only a small part of it, it is still correct to say, "Look, there is the church."[6]

The "local circumscription" sense of the word may be related to geographical areas of different sizes. For example, we find Paul using the term *regionally*, as when he writes of the churches (plural) of Galatia, Macedonia, or Achaia. Thus, each of the Galatian churches appears to have been a free-standing congregation in local circumscription in its own village or community. But the apostle also uses the term *municipally* (e.g. "the church of God that is in Corinth"; 1 Cor 1:2a); *personally* (e.g. in such phrases as "the church of the Thessalonians" [1 Thess 1:1b] where he is clearly thinking of the church as being made up of people); and *locally*, to describe the small house church (e.g. Rom 16:5a, "Greet also the church in their house").

Now, while it is true that groups of the churches are described in the way mentioned above, there is little indication in Scripture of wider organization. In his 1880 Bampton Lectures on *The Organization of the Early Christian Churches*, Dr. Edwin Hatch put it like this:

> Although it is indisputable that our Lord founded a church, it is an unproved assumption that the church is an aggregation of visible and organized societies. The theory upon which the public worship of the primitive churches proceeded was that each community was complete in itself, and that in every act of public worship, every element of the community was present.[7]

 Certainly, as we shall see in chapter 4, the New Testament illustration of the body is much more appropriate in application to a local church, where a member might be an organ or part of a limb, than to the universal church where he would be only an insignificant cell. Certainly the local congregation seems to be the most meaningful unit to us as individuals, for the church universal never meets as such on earth. Newbigin expresses this with characteristic lucidity when he says:

> We must regard the local congregation as having a certain real primacy among the various units into which we may think of the church as being divided. That body of neighbours who share in the same loaf and the same cup, who form the

---

[6] For a qualification of this, see chapter 7 on a definition of the local church: "when is the church not a church?"

[7] Quoted in G.H. Lang, *The Churches of God* (Milton Keynes, United Kingdom: Paternoster Press, 1959), p. 15.

visible company in which the Word is preached, and who, being neighbours, are able in the context of actual personal meeting to build one another up in the faith and to correct one another in love and to wait upon the Lord for his guidance, has a strong claim to be regarded as the primary unit of Christian fellowship.[8]

An Enriched Contemporary Meaning

Two things therefore emerge. First, *ekklēsia* is not an easy word to translate simply into another language, because of its rich background in Israel's history and its derivation implying a group summoned together for a purpose to travel to a destination. Second, in our mental concept of what the church is, we must not think of that which is mainly cultic, such as the performance of a routine of worship in buildings specially set aside for that purpose. Nor must we conceive of the church as just a kind of spiritual club to which we are to some degree "attached" or which we "attend." Rather we must see it as something dynamic and organic into which we are integrated, as we travel together to the same destination and goal.

In each culture we may find a word which expresses something of the essential meaning. It may be a muster, a levy; even, perhaps, a posse where a group is summoned to travel with a common purpose. In some countries the idea of a Great Trek or a Long March may carry the meaning. In the Yao tribal culture, where infertility demands that babies be bought from other tribes and given a new name and new tribal clothes after being chosen by loving parents, the biblical picture of "I and the children God has given me" (Heb 2:13b) may provide a helpful model of the new household of God with its sons by adoption.

In the West we have different problems, but a useful model lies to hand. In an article in the magazine *Japan Harvest* about student unrest in Japan, David Michell wrote, "The church of God is a body which should be demonstrating all the time—demonstrating the love of God." Here the demonstration march becomes a striking picture of what the church is meant to be; the more so if we distinguish between violent, aggressive demonstrations and the "love demo" proposed by Allen Ginsberg in a

---

[8] Newbigin, *Household*, p. 106.

poem he wrote in 1966, called *How to make a March/Spectacle*. Its thesis is that:

> demonstrations should lay aside their usually grave and pug-
> nacious quality in favour of festive dancing and a chanting
> parade, that would pass out balloons and flowers, candy and
> kisses, bread and wine, to everyone along the line of march—
> including any cops or Hell's Angels in the vicinity. The atmo-
> sphere should be one of gaiety and affection governed by the
> intention to attract or seduce participation from the usually
> impassive bystanders—or at least to overcome their worst sus-
> picions and hostilities.[9]

This is a very attractive illustration of the church as a body of people moving together to a specific goal, as well as increasing their numbers along the route.

Theodore Roszak's book is a very interesting one, for when he tries to describe what the New Left or the hippies are looking for, he has to use expressions like "New Jerusalem" or the "Holy City."[10] He actually steals our words! Although it is not what he intends, we could infer from what he says that we, the church of God, are really what young people are look-ing for! The tragedy of the book is that it completely fails to see this. The institutional church has become so disfigured, and the young generation so disenchanted with it, that we have become unrecognizable. This is an issue which we must tackle in this book—how the new community can again become recognizable for what it really is.

President Johnson once called for a "great society." But, with respect, the United States is manifestly not a "great society"—not yet at any rate.

We are! The church of Jesus Christ is the great new society which God is bringing into existence. In Asia we hear of the "new Filipino" and in Japan of the "expected ideal man" (*katai-sareta ningenzoo*); and there is a long-ing in the heart of man worldwide for the ideal new society. The hippies liked to call themselves not only "flower children," but also "the beautiful people." This is what we are! But immediately we have to qualify that by saying, "Well—it is what we are supposed to be." God's purpose is that his church should be a thing of "splendor, without spot or wrinkle or any such thing" (Eph 5:27b). But that is manifestly still future. Nevertheless, it is still the goal of the church.

---

[9] Theodore Roszak, *The Making of a Counter Culture* (New York: Anchor Books, 1968), p. 150.

[10] *Ibid.*, p. 49.

Let me close this section by quoting a poem of Julian Beck that expresses in a purely secular sense the desire for an effective revolutionary movement to change our world, but which finds a response in our hearts as Christians. It describes the kind of new community which the church ought to be becoming now.

we want
to zap them
with holiness

we want
to levitate them
with joy

we want
to open them
with love vessels

we want
to clothe the wretched
with linen and light

we want
to put music and truth
in our underwear

we want
to make the land and its cities glow
with creation

we will make it
irresistible
even to racists…

we want to change
the demonic character of our opponents
into productive glory[11]

The chapters that follow are an attempt to reshape our mental image of the church by recalibrating our thinking against the biblical standards, and then relating them directly to our own practical experience of Christian communal life in the congregation. The neo-Arcadians write so powerfully of the aspirations of youth today for such a new society, a beautiful community.

---

[11] Julian Beck, *Paradise Now: Collective Creation of Living Theatre* (New York: Random House, 1971).

I want us to see that this is biblically the Father's design for the church. This was why Christ gave himself for the church (Eph 5:25ff)—in order to make her beautiful. And this is what the Holy Spirit is seeking to do now, by building us together (Eph 2:21-22) into the new living temple.

I confess that I am really excited about this—and want to share with you this glorious biblical vision of what the people of God is meant to be. But our current practice, and even more our current thinking, places many obstacles in the way of our achieving the divine goal. We turn to a very significant one in the next chapter.

Chapter 2 Salvation More Than Personal

You shall call his name Jesus, for he will save his
people from their sins (Matt 1:21b)

Many of the commonest expressions used in the New Testament to describe the church are plural nouns such as brethren, children, saints, disciples; or collective nouns such as flock, nation, and people. If I underline that these are plural concepts you may wonder why I am laboring the obvious!

The reason is that many Christians in the English-speaking world seem to talk and to think of "salvation" very much as a solitary personal experience. "I am saved," they say; "I am being sanctified," "I am going to heaven," and so on. The attitude of some Christians toward other Christians, and particularly toward active and responsible participation in a particular congregation, suggests that there is something very defective in their highly individualistic view of what "salvation" is all about. This tendency is reflected in the way in which we sing about our faith. This can be demonstrated very simply by picking up any of the popular hymn books in everyday use and noting how very many "I" and "my" hymns there are, and how relatively few "we" and "our" hymns there are, which are really suitable for congregational singing. Most of our hymns would be much more suitable as solos! It is as though most Christians expect to fly solo to heaven with only just a little bit of formation flying from time to time!

The Impossibility of Being a Solitary Saint

How many times does the word "saint" occur in the text of the New Testament? Get hold of a concordance and you will discover that the plural form "saints" occurs some sixty-one times. Only once (Phil 4:21a) is the singular used and that is in the phrase, "Greet every saint"! The concept of a solitary saint is foreign to the New Testament writers. The idea of the hermit of solitary religious recluse, far from being biblical in origin, seems to be more of the product of an escapist type of extreme separatism. Elijah the Tishbite and John the Baptist were certainly ascetics, but neither of them appears to have lived alone as a solitary hermit. Their teaching was attended in the one case by "the school of the prophets" and in the other by "the disciples of John." There would appear to be little biblical justification for our becoming spiritual Robinson Crusoes.

The basic meaning of the word "saint" suggests primarily not so much a holy, moral character, as the fact that saints are "separated," "set apart," or "wholly dedicated" to God. It is because they are his and belong to him that the quality of holy living is expected. Holiness is the product of their being saints, and not the basis of it. Like the faithful Samurai, Japanese retainers of a feudal lord who are utterly committed to their master's cause to the very death, the "saints" are those who are committed unreservedly to Christ as Lord, and who act together corporately in his interest.

Confusions of English Grammar

One possible cultural reason for our Western individualism derives from the fact that in standard English, the second person singular "you" and the second person plural "you" are identical. Thus, New Testament Letters addressed to congregations are read as though they were addressed to individuals. It is good and right that we should apply the Scriptures to ourselves personally, but it is unfortunate if we also apply the Scriptures individualistically and ignore the fact that their original intention was to instruct us not so much as individuals, but as whole communities of Christian people.

The letter to the Ephesians is an exceedingly corporate book all about the church. Yet, to give one amusing example, how frequently we hear expositions of Paul's description of the Christian's armor in Ephesians 6 as a description of the individual, solitary Christian in his lonely, spiritual battle with Apollyon! The idea of a solitary Roman soldier going out all on his own to fight the wild Welsh, Picts, Germans, and Franks is quite ludicrous! They would have made mincemeat of him. The Romans were so effective because they developed to perfection the military art of corporate maneuver so that their huge oblong shields fitted together to make a great wall which their opponents were not able to break. It is perfectly clear in Greek, Chinese, Japanese or any decent language, that the passage concerned is a plural passage containing plural verbs and pronouns; for example, "we do not wrestle" (Eph 6:12a), and "making supplication for all the saints" (Eph 6:18c).

Again, many talks that are given about the work of the Holy Spirit relate almost entirely to his work in the individual believer. Yet many of the references used as proof texts on such occasions will be found to be plural and therefore more appropriate when used of congregations than of the individual. For example, Romans 8:14 and 16 are often quoted as proof texts for individual guidance and assurance, as though they read, "He who is led by the Spirit of God is a son of God...," "The Spirit himself bears witness with my spirit that I am a child of God..." These verses would properly seem to be more appropriate to the corporate guidance and corporate assurance of Christians, but they are frequently quoted in an entirely individual sense. To expound them in the corporate sense might be a healthy corrective to some of the individualistic "I felt led..." type of justification for individualistic action.

Another interesting and highly topical illustration of the same tendency may be seen in current expositions of "Earnestly desire the higher gifts" (1 Cor 12:31a) and "Pursue love, and earnestly desire the spiritual gifts" (1 Cor 14:1a). These Scriptures are commonly expounded to the effect that each individual Christian should seek various spiritual gifts for himself and particularly, perhaps, the gift of speaking in tongues. This interpretation seems to make nonsense of the earlier section in chapter 12, in which Paul's whole point is that different members of the body each have different functions to perform and different contributions to make to the whole body. Once it is appreciated, however, that the Letter to the Corinthians is addressed not to each individual in the congregation separately, but to the Corinthian congregation *as a whole*, we realize that these verses are encouraging us to seek and to pray that *all* the spiritual gifts required for the edification of the corporate body will be exercised by some member of the congregation. It does not encourage us to pray that I, as an individual, may have all the higher gifts, but rather that we as a congregation may have them all. An individualistic interpretation of Scripture is thus responsible, to a certain extent, for some of the distressing controversies which have divided Christians from time to time.

In the past we have rightly needed to re-emphasize, as Evangelicals, the necessity of "personal salvation," "personal experience," and "personal sanctification," because there was a tendency at the time to ignore the preaching of the necessity for each individual to be born again. Of course we *must* be "born again" individually; not as orphans, however, but as members of God's congregational family. At the same time we must not rush to the opposite extreme and become so enthusiastic about corporate and congregational applications of Scripture that we neglect, or underemphasize, the necessity of individual faith and a personal walk with Christ. It is not that we need to substitute a new emphasis for the old one, but that we need to emphasize the corporate alongside the personal.

Thus whenever English readers heard the word "you" in a Letter addressed to one of the New Testament congregations, we need mentally to translate it into the pleasing "you all" of the southern States or even the delightful Ulster colloquial "yous" or "youse'uns!"

Subjectivism Overstressed

Just as we have rightly stressed the personal, but have tended to overlook the equally biblical stress on the corporate and have thus become individualistic in our thinking, so also we have tended to overstress solitary and subjective religious experience and have failed to emphasize the biblical necessity of corporate fellowship in the church. We have stressed private worship in the "quiet time," but public worship has tended to become formal and dead.

There are very real dangers in some of our rather ultra-subjective emphases on individual experience and guidance. It is significant that in the New Testament even prophecy (which could be defined as a direct word from the Lord) must be judged or weighed by others (1 Cor 14:29). How much more do we need today such corporate checks on our guidance, lest we follow what may be only an individual whim or fancy.

For the Buddhist, of course, subjective experience is all there is, because the external world has no objective reference and is only an illusion. All desire for the world of concrete entities must be eliminated. Thus the Buddhist sees the world around him as only a series of sensations flashing across the television screen, as it were, of his sense organs. Only my own solitary experience is real, being part of the impersonal "god" which is the totality of all things.

By contrast the Christian is committed to a worldview which regards others as having objective reality and sees them as people who experience real suffering. Therefore, *in the world* I must work actively on behalf of my neighbor and help him objectively. Equally *in the congregation* I must recognize my own personal inadequacy and my need for my brethren, recognizing that God is concerned not only about saving *me* but about saving *us*, the whole body of Christian people, his saints, his people.

The Church is not Merely a Means of Grace

Sometimes the teaching given to new Christians appears to imply that the church is merely an incidental aid to assist the individual in his own personal salvation. It is regarded as just one among a number of means of grace to help us as individuals to grow in grace and knowledge of the Lord Jesus. We tell young converts that, in order to grow, they need to read their Bibles and pray every day and they need fellowship (to help *you* as an individual!); then it is added, almost as an afterthought, that "going to church" may also be helpful sometimes. "Going to church" may even be regarded as something different from fellowship so that it is thought of primarily in terms of attending services. The explanation of the value of going to church in order to "get spiritual food" often continues with an apology, because we may not find all churches very helpful and very often we may not get much palatable spiritual food either! Admittedly this is something of a caricature, but sometimes one does indeed gain the impression that people are told to go to church for reasons that are somewhat obscure, but are part of a Christian's burdensome duty in putting up with archaic language and antiquated forms and a stereotyped diet of hymn sandwiches.

We have to make it abundantly clear that the church is not a mere, incidental means of grace, but that God has a purpose for the church as such. As Emil Brunner puts it, it should "never be thought of as a means to an end, but as an end in itself."[1]

From the very beginning God has intended not only to save individuals, but to bring into being a whole people, a whole new society of community (see Eph 3:4-6, 9-11).

Ephesians: A Letter About the Church

The whole of the Letter to the Ephesians may be taken as a treatise on corporate salvation. It is a general Letter with a minimum of personal information and an absence of local reference. The words "in Ephesus"

---

[1] Emil Brunner, *The Misunderstanding of the Church* (Cambridge, United Kingdom: Lutterworth Press, 1952), p. 10.

(1:1) are not present in all the oldest manuscripts and it would appear, therefore, to be a circular letter which could be read and enjoyed in any local church situation in the first century, and equally, of course, today.

In the opening chapter we notice at once the plural pronouns and the references to God's will and "our inheritance" (1:14). The great prayer that concludes the chapter is that the congregation as a whole may have their "hearts enlightened" so that "you may know what is the hope to which he has called you" (and we have already seen the relationship of the word "called" to *ekklēsia*,—a hope which is further developed as "the riches of his glorious inheritance in the saints" (1:18c). This is clearly a corporate understanding of salvation. The description of Christ's greatness which follows culminates with the description of him as "head over all things to the church, which is his body" (1:22b-23a).

The next chapter describes what we were as sinners and what we have now become by grace, having been "made alive together" (2:1, 5; NKJV). This is a compound verb with the prefix *syn* (as in English words derived from Greek like synthesis, symphony, *etc.*), and it seems to include the idea of being raised together with one another as well as with Christ. The chapter then goes on to describe how, as Gentiles, we were excluded from participation in the "commonwealth of Israel" (2:12b) and how Christ's atoning work has broken down the barrier of the dividing wall between Jews and Gentiles, bringing into existence "a single new humanity" (2:15, NEB). Because of what Christ has done, Jews and Gentiles are now reconciled together in one body. There follows the glorious conclusion: "So then you (plural!) are no longer strangers and aliens (*i.e.* foreigners), but you are fellow citizens with the saints and members of the household of God" (2:19). Paul then continues with the picture of the church as a new temple in which we are being "joined together" (2:21b) and "built together" (two more compound verbs with *syn*) into a new temple for a dwelling place of God. This is the work of the Holy Spirit (2:22b).

In chapter 3, Paul describes the doctrine of this international church as a "mystery of Christ, which was not made known to the sons of men in other generations as it has now been revealed to his holy apostles and prophets by the Spirit. This mystery is that the Gentiles are fellow heirs, members of the same body, and partakers of the promise in Christ Jesus through the gospel" (3:4b-6). Here the apostle uses again three nouns compounded with *syn*. We are heirs together, members of the body together, and partakers of the promise together. Paul coins, in fact, an entirely new word (*synsōma*), found in no other writer, expressing this idea in one word as perhaps we might do in English if we coined the new word

συγκληρονόμος, σύσσωμος, συμμέτοχος
↳ Belong to the same body

"concorporate." The purpose of all this is so that "*through the church* the manifold wisdom of God might now be made known to the rulers and authorities in the heavenly places" (3:10, emphasis added).

The great prayer which follows is once again not so much a prayer for individuals as a prayer that Christians together in the congregation may be strengthened by God's power, know the indwelling of Christ in the congregation, and "comprehend with all the saints" (3:18b) the wonder of the love of Christ. The closing doxology again significantly prays, "to him be glory in the church and in Christ Jesus throughout all generations" (3:21a).

These verses alone, I believe, are sufficient to show that the doctrine of the church in the New Testament is not some peripheral matter of interest merely to theologians, bit is *an essential part of the Christian gospel*. It is indeed wonderful and marvelous enough that we should be remade and recreated as new individuals. What is even more wonderful is the fact that God reconciles us together as a new humanity and forms us into a new community of his people. It is the bringing into existence of this new covenant community which properly ought to be called "God's plan of salvation."

This can be a revolutionary viewpoint for some Christians. All at once the church becomes important, something to work for and to live for because this is what God intends, what God is working for, and we want to see glory brought to him in the church. We suddenly see that the church is intended to be a developing community, a "colony of heaven" on earth. The very mention of the word "saints" immediately suggests "sanctification" and we realize that not only as individuals are we intended to be moving and progressing towards an individual goal of personal holiness, but also that God has planned a corporate congregational sanctification for the whole body of his people.

Selah![2]

It is not enough, then, that I should seek and pray for my own growth and development as an individual. "We are members one of another" (Eph 4:25c, which Phillips translates as "We are not separate units"). I suddenly realize that there is a goal of congregational development and progress, which I may have been almost entirely overlooking. I had thought of the church primarily as something that will sometimes be of help to *me*. Now I begin to realize that I have tremendous responsibilities

---

[2] This word, where it occurs in the Psalms, is a musical direction which would seem to indicate a pause. Just stop a moment to think of the wonderful plan of God for his people!

to the congregation, because all of us are supposed to be developing and progressing together as a wonderful new community of God's people.

His People

The concept of "the people of God" is a fundamental one in our understanding of both the Old and New Testaments. The Old Testament usage will help us to understand the New Testament development of the same thought.

> Old Testament faith knows nothing, in any situation or at any time, of a religious individualism which gives a man a private relationship with God unconnected with the community either in its roots, its realization or its goal. Just as it is the formation of a divine *society* which gives meaning to the divine demand that summons the individual and enlists him in its service, so it is in serving his brethren that the obedience of the one who is called is proved, it is in the common cultic festivals that his religious life finds its natural expression, and it is toward a perfected people of God that his hope is directed.[3]

One wonders how much modification this remarkable statement requires as far as the New Testament is concerned.

The first reference to the people of God in the New Testament is found in the verse which heads this chapter. Again and again we have heard this verse read as part of the Christmas story and recognized that the name Jesus is deeply significant as describing the one who has come to save us from sin. We may well have failed to notice that there is here the first reference in the New Testament not only to sin and to the Savior but also to the church. For he has come to "save his people from their sins" (Matt 1:21b). Lest we should think this reference applies only to the Jewish people, let us remind ourselves of James' summing up at the Council of Jerusalem when he says, "Simeon has related how God first visited the Gentiles, to take from them *a people for his name*" (Acts 15:14, emphasis added); and then goes on to prove that this was always God's plan by quoting Amos 9:11, 12 (see Acts 15:14-18).

In the birth narratives in the Gospels, the angels speaking to Joseph, to Zachariah, and to the shepherds all mention the concept of "his people" as

---

[3] Walter Eichrodt, *The Theology of the Old Testament*, Vol. II (Louisville, KY: Westminster John Knox Press, 1967), p. 265.

also does the Holy Spirit speaking through both Zachariah and Simeon. Thus the angel tells Zachariah that his son John will "make ready for the Lord a people prepared" (Luke 1:17c) while Zachariah himself, filled with the Holy Spirit, prophesies of the unborn Jesus that the Lord God of Israel "has visited and redeemed *his people*" (Luke 1:68, emphasis added) by raising up salvation in the house of David. Turning, then, to his own new-born baby John, he says that he is to "give knowledge of salvation to *his people* in the forgiveness of their sins" (Luke 1:77, emphasis added). The angel's message to the shepherds abiding in the field is "good news of great joy that will be for *all the people*…" (Luke 2:10b, emphasis added) and when the aged Simeon comes into the temple he prophesies in the power of the Spirit concerning "your salvation that you have prepared in the presence of *all peoples*, a light for revelation to the Gentiles, and for glory to your people Israel" (Luke 2:31, 32, emphasis added), indicating an outreach far beyond Israel itself.

In his first Letter, Peter makes great use of "the people" theme. It is particularly interesting in view of all that the Roman church has made of Christ's response to Peter's confession, "On this rock I will build my church" (Matt 16:18b), that in his Letters Peter never once uses the word "church" at all. What he does say is, "you are a chosen race, a royal priesthood, a holy nation, a people for his own possession" (1 Peter 2:9a, quoting Exod 19:5b-6a: "You shall be my treasured possession among all peoples, for all the earth is mine; and you shall be to me a kingdom of priests and a holy nation," and Deut 7:6, "For you are a people holy to the Lord your God. The Lord your God has chosen you to be a people for his treasured possession, out of all the peoples who are on the face of the earth").

Here, verses which originally referred specifically to Israel are now being applied to the new people of God, the church.[4] Paul also echoes these same scriptures when he speaks of God's purpose to "purify for himself a people for his own possession" (Titus 2:14b). Both Paul and Peter quote Hosea 2:23: "I will say to Not my people, 'You are my people'" (Rom 9:25; 1 Peter 2:10a).

The Bible is divided into the old covenant and the new covenant. The new covenant is of course mentioned in the old covenant (see Jer 31:31ff.). Thus, Paul quotes the terms of the new covenant; "I will be their God, and they shall be my people" (2 Cor 6:16b). Many more verses could be

---

[4] Editor's note: For an explanation on the New Testament application of Old Testament passages, see *Let the Text Speak: An Introduction to Biblical Hermeneutics* by Grant Hawley with Jeremy Edmondson (Allen, TX: Bold Grace Ministries, 2018), pp. 24-26.

cited, but it ought to be clear that the *salvation of a people* has always been, and still is, according to Scripture, the great purpose of God.

We have already seen in the first chapter that the very concept of "people" reminds us that the church has a goal and a destination towards which it is travelling. This idea is expressed in Ephesians 4:13a: "Until we all attain to the unity of the faith…". "Attain" translates a word meaning "arrive at," used eight times in Acts of travelers arriving at their destination. If we recognize that the church is God's travelling people, then our eyes are focused on our future destination. God has brought into existence a new saved community, a "caravan," a new "summoned out" people travelling together to a destination.

Alan Stibbs, in his book *God's Church*, points out how, as early as Exodus 6:7, God declares, "I will take you to be my people, and I will be your God," and that equally in the closing chapters of Revelation, in the description of the holy city, the new Jerusalem coming down out of heaven, we meet the same reference; "they will be his people" (Rev 21:3b). I cannot do better than to sum this up in Alan Stibbs's own words: "It is therefore God's unmistakable purpose to have a people of his own, and by his amazing grace it is the utterly undeserved privilege of all who belong to Christ to belong to this community, the people of God."[5] This is something to get excited about.

Getting Down to Brass Tacks

> All your patient sees (writes Uncle Screwtape to Wormwood) is the half-finished, sham Gothic erection on the new building estate. When he goes inside, he sees the local grocer with rather an oily expression on his face bustling up to offer him one shiny little book containing a liturgy which neither of them understands, and one shabby little book containing corrupt texts of a number of religious lyrics, mostly bad, and in very small print. When he gets to his pew and looks around him he sees just that selection of his neighbours whom he has hitherto avoided. You want to lean pretty heavily on those neighbours. Make his mind flit to and fro between an expression like "the body of Christ" and the actual faces in the next pew. It matters very little, of course, what kind of people that next pew really contains. You may know one of

---

[5] Alan M. Stibbs, *God's Church* (Downers Grove, IL: IVP, 1959), p. 10.

them to be a great warrior on the Enemy's side. No matter. Your patient, thanks to Our Father below, is a fool. Provided that any of those neighbours sing out of tune, or have boots that squeak, or double chins, or odd clothes, the patient will quite easily believe that their religion must therefore be somehow ridiculous. At his present stage, you see, he has an idea of "Christians" in his mind which he supposes to be spiritual but which, in fact, is largely pictorial. His mind is full of togas and sandals and armour and bare legs, and the mere fact that the other people in church wear modern clothes is a real—though of course an unconscious—difficulty to him. Never let it come to the surface; never let him ask what he expected them to look like.[6]

This may seem like coming down from the sublime to the ridiculous. But it seems important that we, too, should face the relationship between the biblical teaching and the local congregation which I hope we do not merely "attend," or are loosely "attached to," but to which we may say with all our hearts and with a new depth of meaning, "I belong!" If what we have been saying in these chapters is correct, we have to begin to look at the apparently unprepossessing group, the congregation to which we belong, in an entirely new light.

---

[6] C.S. Lewis, *The Screwtape Letters* (New York: MacMillan Company, 1942), p. 15-16.

Chapter 3 - Salvation Under Construction

You are… God's building project. (1 Cor 3:9, my translation)

Even when God's people were represented only by Abraham and those with him they are not to be thought of merely as an aggregation of wandering nomads in the wilderness. Abraham might have lived in tents like Isaac and Jacob, but it is said of him that "he was looking forward to the city that has foundations, whose designer and builder is God" (Heb 11:10). Similarly, the patriarchs are described as those who are seeking a country of their own. "They desire a better country, that is, a heavenly one. Therefore, God is not ashamed to be called their God, for he has prepared for them a city (Heb 11:16). And later, the same writer, exhorting the suffering Jewish Christians to continue, encourages them by saying, "For here we have no lasting city, but we seek the city that is to come" (Heb 13:14).

Once one becomes aware of this, one suddenly begins to discover that this corporate theme of God's community is to be found everywhere in the Bible. There is a future, coming, heavenly city. It is described earlier in the Letter to the Hebrews as "the world to come" (2:5b), and the word used here suggests "the civilized world to come." Thus, among all the writer's many other plural references to "many sons" (2:10b), "brothers" (2:11c), "the congregation" (2:12b), "children" (2:13b), "the people" (2:17c), there are these striking references to the new city for which all the Old Testament saints were looking. We have already noted the borrowing of Christian terms by neo-Arcadians like Roszak to describe the Utopia for which they are seeking. Let us be clear, then, that as Christians we are looking for a new heaven and a new earth and for "the holy city, new Jerusalem" (Rev 21:2a). The vagrant, itinerant life of the patriarchs and the wandering people of God on their way to the promised land always had in view the ultimate building of the city of God which is to be called "The Lord is there" (Ezek 48:35c).

The salvation which God has planned, then, is not merely aimed at producing saved individuals. We are looking for a wonderful new community and a truly great society, God's own people. In our impatience and rebellion against the institutional church we must not throw out the biblical baby with the institutional bath water.

In biblical thinking, salvation is not merely plural, but Christians are to be brought together as living stones and put together into a new building in which God is to be worshipped, a new and glorious structure. There is all the difference in the world between a great heap of bricks and those same bricks carefully fitted together and built into a beautifully designed building.

The Ugly Building Site

How foolish a tourist visiting a growing Asian city such as Singapore would be if he complained about the great eyesores, the huge heaps of scaffolding with cranes on top, and the need to pick one's way painfully across the ugly boards and the dirty pavements. We might well rebuke him for being so stupidly shortsighted! "Just wait a few weeks, will you? The building isn't finished yet! But the day is fixed when this beautiful building will be completed. And when all the scaffolding is taken down and the site cleared up, it's going to be the most beautiful building you've ever seen. Just look at these plans, and see what it's going to be like!"

Similarly, the new building of God is still under construction. And we should be most foolish if we disregarded the church because of its present imperfections. It is a peculiarity of our individualistic thinking that we are prepared to tolerate all manner of imperfections in ourselves as individuals and yet feel free to criticize the churches for their congregational imperfections. Logically, we ought to extend to the group of Christians the same measure of tolerance and patience as that which we expect those Christians to extend towards us as inconsistent and imperfect individuals.

We have seen already that the church is made up of people who are sinners saved by grace, and those who formerly were outsiders, strangers, and foreigners, who through Christ's reconciling work have been brought into the new body (Eph 2). If the church is made up of people like this, we should certainly anticipate trouble! If you are building a new community out of sinful men and women, you are foolishly idealistic if you expect to get away without problems arising. As the Puritan Richard Baxter once said, "The church on earth is a mere hospital!"[1] Those of us who have been admitted as in-patients have come within its walls precisely because we are sinners in need of treatment. The doctor on his ward round does not castigate the recently admitted patient because he is not yet fully recovered. He came to the hospital because he needed treatment. It would be very foolish to criticize hospitals as ineffective because their inmates are sick!

There is a very real danger that we may thoughtlessly build up a mental image of a perfect New Testament church which never in fact existed. We have the New Testament Letters precisely because New Testament congregations were distinctly imperfect and therefore required rebuke and corrective teaching. The Galatians were wrong on a basic point of doctrine. The Philippians were suffering from disunity. The Colossians were suffering from a group within the church who regarded themselves as better than everybody else because they had embraced a special new teaching. And Corinth had all manner of problems—problems of immorality, of factions in the congregation, and even unsoundness on such a basic doctrine as that of the resurrection of the dead.

The Sinfulness and Fallibility of the Church

"The face of the church is the face of the sinner," said Luther; which suggests that Protestants, at any rate, are perfectly clear about the fallibility of the church as a human institution.

> No honest person can deny that the church as a visible institution has, in the course of its history, been guilty of pride, greed, sloth and culpable blindness. Nor can we admit the possibility of easing the difficulty by making a radical distinction between the church and its members. The "individual Christian" is such only as a member of Christ, and there is no meaning in saying that the body of Christ cannot sin but his members can. Nor, finally, does the New Testament leave us in any doubt that the church *does* sin. The words, "Ye are the body of Christ" and the words, "Ye are yet carnal," were addressed by the same apostle to the same body of men and women. The living Lord of the church can say to a church, "I know thy works, that thou hast the name that thou livest, and

---

[1] Richard Baxter, William Orme, *The Practical Works of the Rev. Richard Baxter: With a Life of the Author, and a Critical Examination of His Writings*, Volume 22 (London: Mills, Jowett, and Mills, 1830), p. 160.

thou are dead." The Lord himself can remove the candlestick out of its place.[2]

Just as we are familiar with the conflict between spirit and flesh in the life of the individual believer, we should be quite wrong to deny that a similar conflict goes on in the life of the church.

> The problem of how an unholy concourse of sinful men and women can be in truth the body of Christ is the same as the problem of how a sinful man can at the same time be accepted as a child of God… Our present situation arises precisely from the fact that this fundamental insight which the Reformers apply to the position of the Christian man was not followed through in its application to the nature of the Christian church.[3]

We should not, therefore, allow ourselves to be turned off by the church because it manifests its imperfections so blatantly. It is exactly the same problem as that of the imperfections of the individual believer. We know that the Holy Spirit is working in us as individuals to transfigure us into the likeness of Christ. Perhaps we should notice that 2 Corinthians 3:18—"And we all, with unveiled face, beholding the glory of the Lord, are being transformed into the same image from one degree of glory to another. For this comes from the Lord who is the Spirit"—is a plural reference. The same Spirit is working in the church also, so that we are brought to the beauty of moral excellence and also, intellectually, to doctrinal truth.

The building is still under construction. It is not yet finished, and the fact of its imperfection should be clearly recognized and accepted. We are foolish to expect to find anywhere a perfected congregation at this stage. Nonetheless, God's aim to prefect and finish the building is equally clear in Scripture.

The New Temple in Building

It was in days when the first Christians were still making regular daily visits to the Jerusalem Temple that that exceedingly brilliant Christian, Stephen, whose beautiful life was cut short so abruptly, saw most clearly what God was going to do. Stephen was accused of saying that Jesus "will

---

[2] Newbigin, *The Household of God*, p. 81.

[3] *Ibid.*, p. 29.

destroy this place" (Acts 6:14b) and in significant quotations from the Old Testament he reminded the Jews of God's eternal purpose.

> Yet the Most High does not dwell in houses made by hands, as the prophet says,
>
> "Heaven is my throne, and the earth is my footstool."
>
> "What kind of house will you build for me," says the Lord, "or what is the place of my rest?
>
> Did not my hand make all these things?"
> (Acts 7:48-50, quoting Isa 66:1, 2)

This point seems to have penetrated at last the minds of the other Christians of the Jerusalem church after the persecution which followed Stephen's martyrdom. Thus, in the Jerusalem Council, when James spoke of God concerning himself about taking from among the nations "a people for his name," he goes on to say,

> And with this the words of the prophets agree, just as it is written,
> "After this I will return,
> and I will rebuild the tent of David that has fallen;
> I will rebuild its ruins,
> and I will restore it,
> that the remnant of mankind may seek the Lord,
> and all the Gentiles who are called by my name,"
> says the Lord, who makes these things known from of old.
> (Acts 15:15-18, quoting from Amos 9:11, 12)

Similarly, Peter develops this picture:

> As you come to him, a living stone rejected by men but in the sight of God chosen and precious, you yourselves like living stones are being built up as a spiritual house, to be a holy priesthood, to offer spiritual sacrifices acceptable to God through Jesus Christ (1 Pet 2:4-5).

It is not surprising, therefore, that Paul also develops the same idea in his Letter to the Ephesians:

> You are... built on the foundation of the apostles and prophets, Christ Jesus himself being the cornerstone, in whom the whole structure, being joined together, grows into a holy temple in the Lord. In him you also are being built together

into a dwelling place for God by the Spirit (Eph 2:19a,
20-22).

Here, then, is the tremendous purpose of the new temple which God is
building, not out of dead stones, but out of living people. Forgive me for
quoting so many verses but it is helpful for us to realize how widespread
this picture of the church is in Scripture. "We are the temple of the living
God" (2 Cor 6:16b).

There is an even longer passage in the first Letter to the Corinthians,
from which the rather freely translated text at the head of this chapter is
taken. The force of the word translated "building," like the word translated "field" in the same verse, is not merely the static harvest field or
building, so much as the whole process of husbandry (the agricultural
project) and the whole process of building (God's building project). Paul
continues:

> According to the grace of God given to me, like a skilled
> master builder I laid a foundation, and someone else is build-
> ing upon it. Let each one take care how he builds upon it.
> For no one can lay a foundation other than that which is laid,
> which is Jesus Christ. Now if anyone builds on the founda-
> tion with gold, silver, precious stones, wood, hay, straw—
> each one's work will become manifest, for the Day will dis-
> close it, because it will be revealed by fire, and the fire will test
> what sort of work each one has done. If the work that anyone
> has built on the foundation survives, he will receive a reward.
> If anyone's work is burned up, he will suffer loss, though he
> himself will be saved, but only as through fire.
>
> Do you not know that you are God's temple and that God's
> Spirit dwells in you? If anyone destroys God's temple, God
> will destroy him. For God's temple is holy, and you are that
> temple (1 Cor 3:10-17).

It is particularly interesting to notice the differing stress between the
agricultural and architectural metaphors which Paul employs. In the
picture of the unharvested fields all the emphasis is on God's sovereignty.
The whole agricultural project is his. The workers are his; he provides
the seed they sow, and the water with which they irrigate. It is only God
himself who can give the proper growth. In the architectural metaphor,
however, the stress moves in a very marked way from divine sovereignty
to human responsibility. It is not only that the field is not harvested, but
the building is not finished.

But we are responsible to *be careful how we build*. We must not mess about with the only sound foundation. It is frightening to see how much liberty divine sovereignty has allowed to us men to interfere with the building of his church. There is the terrible possibility that we may be shoddy jerry-builders, building with wood, hay, and straw. The famous story of "The Three Little Pigs," so charmingly cartooned by Walt Disney, has real application here. It is possible in a missionary situation to build a congregation on generous handouts and material incentives. Those whose idea of missionary work is restricted to making material provision seem blind to the fact that these people may not really be converted to Christianity but to Western scientific materialism and its benefits! When the Big Bad Wolf appears, and huffs and puffs, the house of straw will collapse. It is equally possible or a work to be built around an attractive personality and again this may prove to be a house of sticks which the Enemy may destroy. Here is a solemn warning to "be careful how we build." Scripture apparently is not just interested in our having entertaining services which are well attended, nor even in mere evangelism which brings individuals into an experience of Christ but fails to build them into a living community.

The Demolition of the Church

The question arises of what Paul means when he speaks of somebody who "destroys God's temple" (1 Cor 3:17a), especially in view of Christ's words, "I will build my church; and the gates of hell shall not prevail against it" (Matt 16:18b). C. K. Barrett helpfully comments, "Paul is thinking of a local manifestation of God's temple, a local church: and it is a matter of fact that local churches have, under various pressures, including that of heresy, simply gone out of existence."[4] He goes on to draw attention to the prophetic warnings to the seven churches of Asia Minor (see especially Rev 2:5; 3:16). It would seem that these churches failed to heed the Lord's warning, for in fact the seven churches, including the church of Ephesus where Paul first labored, to which at least one copy of the Letter we call "Ephesians" went, and where Timothy subsequently ministered, ultimately went out of existence. It is a solemn and sobering fact. Someone was responsible for destroying the temple of God. At the time of writing there are probably not more than about a hundred Turkish Christians. Yet the Letters to the Galatians, Colossians, and Ephesians, as well as the letters to the seven churches, were all addressed to congregations in the

---

4 C. K. Barrett, *The First Epistle to the Corinthians* (New York: Harper & Row, 1971), p. 91.

geographical area which is now Turkey. It even includes Cilicia in which lay Paul's birth place, Tarsus.

We need this solemn reminder, then, that churches are not only fallible but also demolishable. It is not only possible for a congregation to progress and advance in corporate sanctification, but it is also possible for it to regress, grow cold, apostasize, and disappear.

The Certainty of Completion

The former gloomy reminder needs to be offset by a fresh expression of faith in Christ's promise: "I will build my church; and the gates of hell shall not prevail against it" (Matt 16:18b), which is a clear reference to the universal church.

Certainly, some individual congregations, and even whole denominations and groups of churches, may become formal and perish. In tropical countries we are very familiar with ferns where there are always dying branches on the outside of the spiral which are falling away. But equally there is always new and fresh growth springing up in the center. In the same way God is always at work to bring into existence new and fresh life in the churches.

At a meeting in 1973 with some German missionaries, many of them asked me about the sad situation in post-Christian Europe where the church seems to be in regress. I reminded them of all that had happened in the previous 168 years. On April 7, 1805 Henry Martyn preached his farewell sermon in Holy Trinity Church, Cambridge, on the text "I will build thee an house" (2 Sam 7:27, AV). Martyn's voyage carried him as far as the West Indies and almost to South America. In 1805 there was, as far as I am aware, no Protestant missionary work at all in the whole of that continent. Martyn travelled on with a British fleet which captured the Cape from the Dutch, and which also gave him an opportunity to meet the missionary Dr. van der Kemp and some of the baptized Hottentot Christians there. Apart from the community of liberated Christian slaves at Freetown and the Coptic church of Ethiopia, these were probably the only Christians in the whole of Africa. Livingstone had not even been born at that time.

Martyn then went on to India, and one begins to realize how very few Protestant missionaries, let alone Christians, there were in the whole of Asia. The remarkably sacrificial evangelistic work done by Roman Catholic missionaries in China, Japan, and Korea had been almost totally wiped out. Notices banning Christianity were up in Japan and Korea. Two years would pass before Morrison would gain a foothold in Canton. It was 1813 before Judson reached Burma and Robinson and Bruckner began work in Java. Missionary work had yet to begin in New Zealand. Melbourne did not exist. Nor did Singapore. There were as yet no North American missionary societies at all. There were the German missionaries in India sent out by the King of Denmark and there were the Syrian Christians in South India. There were, of course, some Dutch Christians and a handful of converts in Ceylon and among Eurasians in Java.

Today[5] there are said to be fifteen million evangelical Christians in Latin America, twenty million in Africa, while in Asia the Church of Indonesia alone claims five or six million members and the Church of Korea more than two million. And all this has happened in the equivalent of two long lifetimes of eighty-four years. Perhaps this will encourage us as we see that "the full number of the Gentiles" (Rom 11:25c) is being brought in and that Christ is building his church as he promised.

Building continues.

Accepting Responsibility for the Church

How do we apply this teaching of the importance of building the new temple? How does our expectation of the new city become relevant to us now? There is always a danger that, as Christians, we may be merely passive spectators instead of active participators. Any fool can shout abuse and offer unsolicited advice from the touchline. What we need are Christians who will get their heads into the church scrum and shove!

When the church in Philippi was experiencing various problems, Paul wrote to tell them that they were responsible for putting the congregation right again; using the famous words, "Work out your own salvation with fear and trembling" (Phil 2:12b). "Salvation" has become such a piece of Christian jargon that we fail to appreciate what this verse says. In the first century the word had a much wider and more general meaning of rescue, deliverance, and recovery, as well as referring to Christians' being delivered from the penalty, power, and presence of sin. A typical "get well card" on first-century papyrus would read, "I have heard that you are ill and I am praying for your salvation…," i.e., your recovery. The word is used freely in Acts 27, describing a purely physical rescue from shipwreck. In the first chapter of the same Letter to the Philippians Paul says that

---

[5] That is, when this book was originally published in 1973.

their "prayers and the help of the Spirit" will work out for his "salvation" (Phil 1:19b). He does not mean, of course, that he is not yet converted. He is, however, in prison and under possible sentence of execution, and thus he believes that through their prayers and God's enabling he will be delivered from his present situation, either by release from prison, or if that is God's will, through a victorious imprisonment and triumphant death into everlasting glory.

The context of our quotation from Philippians 2 suggests that the Christians were not of the same mind and of the same love, were not in full accord, and were in danger of doing things out of selfishness and conceit, and in their own interest. They needed to recognize that they belonged to a group bound by ties of love participating together as a holy temple indwelt by the Holy Spirit (Phil 2:1-3). Therefore, Paul says, work out your own deliverance, the solution of your present problems, and bring the congregation back to full health. Some people might not wish to accept this responsibility and might want to leave it till Paul came. Paul therefore urges "not only as in my presence but much more in my absence, work out your own salvation…". Other quietists do not wish to take action but wish to "leave it to the Lord." Paul will not let them escape so easily. "You are responsible," he says in effect, "to work out your own salvation, for God is at work in you, both to will and to work for his good pleasure." In other words, it is God himself who makes you responsible for the work of the church. It does no good when people sit back and criticize the church as though they bore no responsibility for its defects. If there is something wrong with the church then we must accept responsibility and do our utmost to put it right. I sometimes ask young people to express in a sentence the kind of church to which they belong. All I am primarily interested in is the initial pronoun. If they refer to the congregation as "it" or "they," then their whole attitude is deficient and irresponsible! We must be prepared to use the word "we" of the congregation. It is no good being disinterested and detached, just objective and critical observers. We must be intimately involved and fully integrated into the congregation.

When Paul met the Ephesian elders for the last time he told them that they must be responsible for the congregation: "Pay careful attention to yourselves and to all the flock, in which the Holy Spirit has made you overseers, to care for the church of God, which he obtained with his own blood" (Acts 20:28). Certainly it is God's church and it is the word of God and the grace of God which are "able to build you up and give you the inheritance among all those who are sanctified" (Acts 20:32b). But he uses human agents to build the church. We therefore have a double responsibility, not only to look for the blessing which will come to us from God through other believers, but also to be certain that blessing is flowing from God through us to other believers.

There is a striking illustration in the Old Testament where the prophets Haggai, Zechariah, and Malachi speak the word of God to the people about their present failures. They are failing to build the Temple of God. They are despising the worship of God; there are all manner of corruptions among Levitical priesthood, including divorce and neglect of their marriage partners, and the people are failing to give of their substance in tithing for the Temple because they are so disenchanted with it. Then it is the men of action, Ezra and Nehemiah, who act upon the prophets' words and implement the necessary reformation. Here are men who cared and who took action on behalf of the people of God, and the city of God.

Will you do the same?

There is an interesting challenge in the pessimistic comment of Theodore Roszak:

> Yet what else but such a brave (and hopefully humane) perversity can pose a radical challenge to the technocracy? If the melancholy history of revolution over the past half century teaches us anything, it is the futility of a politics which concentrates itself single-mindedly on the overthrowing of governments, or ruling classes, or economic systems. This brand of politics finishes with merely redesigning the turrets and towers of the technocratic citadel. It is the foundations of the edifice that must be sought. And those foundations lie among the ruins of the visionary imagination and the sense of human community.[6]

There is something else besides this "brave perversity" which can "pose a radical challenge to the technocracy."

We can.

With our vision of the holy city and the human community which is God's church.

---

[6] Roszak, *The Making of a Counter Culture*, p. 55.

Chapter 4- Salvation Corporate and Co-Operative

Now you are the body of Christ and individually
members of it. (1 Cor 12:27)

The expression "body," in terms of occurrences and the number of verses in which it is found, is by far the commonest metaphor for the church found in the New Testament. The key passages are Romans 12:4, 5, where we are reminded that there are many members in one body; 1 Corinthians 10:16, 17, and 11:29, where we are told in the context of teaching regarding the Lord's supper that we are one loaf and one body; and 1 Corinthians 12:12-27 where the analogy is worked out in detail with no less than seventeen references to the word. In addition, there are a further seven references in Ephesians and five in Colossians. Because this is the commonest illustration used to help us to understand the nature of the church we need to give it careful attention.

The Origin of the Illustration

Where did Paul get this illustration from? Unlike all the other illustrations for the church, this one has no linguistic roots in the Old Testament (though we find a collective Israel and hints of a corporate Servant). Moreover, there is no derivation possible from the Gospels or from Acts. This is understandable, because the focus of the pre-Pentecostal experience of the disciples was upon Christ in the flesh, dwelling among us (John 1:14). Paul probably gained it from his conversations with Dr. Luke. It is interesting that, as well as his allusions to the parts that make up the joints

(Eph 4:16, Col 2:19), written at a time when we know that "the beloved physician" was with him (Col 4:14), he uses in Ephesians 4:12 the word *katartismos* (translated by RSV as "equipment"), employed by the Greek physician Galen as a technical word for the reduction of dislocations and fractures, so that its use in the "body" context is surely significant.[1]

The Body: Universal or Local?

It is arguable that both in Ephesians and Colossians, "the church which is his body" means the worldwide or universal church made up of both Jews and Gentiles, and having cosmic significance. In Romans and Corinthians, however, it would seem to be the local congregation which is likened to a body made up of different limbs and organs. The picture of a body with its limbs seems somewhat inappropriate and difficult to apply practically to a body with quite so many members and parts to it as the universal church.[2] It would seem to be an anachronism to expect an illustration based on cells and molecules, and the apostle never does it. He does talk about a body made up of hands, feet, eyes and ears, and this seems much more applicable to the local congregation and its relationships than to the church universal.[3] While some of us might in all humility be able to see ourselves as hands and feet, or yet more modestly as fingers and toes of a small, local congregational body, any individual who claimed to be a foot of the church universal might rightly be regarded as too big for his boots! It could also be argued that, as the Letter to the Ephesians was to be read in various separate congregations (the universal church "in local circumscription"), its hearers might well apply its teaching on "the church" to themselves in their local congregation rather than to the larger body they had never seen. The closing references to "the church" in Colossians are certainly entirely local (Col 4:15, 16). To say this is not to deny the validity of the universal church being the body of Christ, but only to suggest that its value as an illustration is primarily of local application.

---

[1] In view of considerable scholarship devoted to working out the relationships between the sacramental and mystical "body" of Christ, this may seem to some to be theologically naïve and oversimplified, but see this chapter, under the heading "The Meaning of the Body of Christ," # 4. J.A.T. Robinson summarizes no less than five possible origins for the concept of the body, none of which is the simple one suggested here. See *The Body: A Study in Pauline Theology* (Chicago: Henry Regnery, 1952), p. 55ff.

[2] Robert Brow, *The Church: An Organic Picture of Its Life and Mission* (Grand Rapids, MI: Eerdmans, 1968).

[3] Who wants to be a cell in the gluteus muscle of the church universal?!

The Meaning of the Body of Christ

1. The term can mean, first, *the body of Christians*; that is, it describes merely a collection of people. It certainly means this and includes this, but the Bible talks of the "body of Christ" rather than "the body of Christians." Thus, we must go much further than this.

2. Second, it means *the society which belongs to Christ*. This is interpreting the genitive "of Christ" as referring to possession. It is the body of believers who belong to him.

3. Third, it means *the organism which is organically united with Christ.* The "body" is organically united together as an organism and not merely collected together in a society. A congregation is more than an aggregation. We recognize that we are joined to Christ by faith and that we are abiding in him. Therefore, we are united together in his body with others who are also joined to him and abiding in him.

4. Some would go further and interpret the term as meaning *the organism which may be identified with Christ*. They argue that the word is not used just figuratively or as an illustration, but that Christians together as his church are literally his body. Thus Professor C.F.D. Moule says, "Christians are not the body of Christians, nor merely limbs of one another (though that they are), but the body and limbs of Christ."[4] He goes on to talk of Paul's making a daring leap from the concept of their being nourished by the body of Christ "to this conception of their actually being Christ's body." Those who take the picture thus far think of the church on earth as Christ's body continuing to be incarnate on earth. This is developed into the so-called "incarnation theology" beloved of ecumenical theologians, often with the further complication of sacramental ideas. This raises all manner of problems, not least of which is to know whether we are to identify "the body" with any existing organizational structure, or whether this is an "invisible" concept. To me it seems to be pressing a helpful analogy far too far, and dangerously so. As the Reformers denied Christ's corporeal presence on earth in the face of false sacramentalism, so we should deny his incarnate presence on earth today in the face of a false ecclesiasticism.

---

4 C.F.D. Moule, Cambridge Greek Text Commentary, *Colossians*, (Cambridge, England: Cambridge University Press, 1968), p.6.

This book is pressing the importance of the doctrine of the church upon a generation which has neglected and undervalued it. But that does not mean that we should therefore overstate the importance and authority of the church. It does not seem to me that biblically we can go so far as to say that the church is literally an extension of the incarnation.[5] We must surely insist that the picture of the body is one helpful metaphor among a number in the New Testament, but that when pressed to extremes it can be misleading. For example, it could be argued that, if the church is a bride who reaches her fullest beauty on the day of her wedding with the Lamb, subsequently she will grow old and grey and lose her beauty. Obviously this would be foolishly pressing the illustration too far. It would seem to be an equally gratuitous and dangerous extrapolation of biblical teaching to talk of the church on earth as being literally an extension of the incarnation. How could such a literal incarnation of Jesus also be his bride?

The church on earth is an exceedingly fallible body made up of fallible human beings.[6] Church history surely makes that abundantly clear! The church as a body is neither inerrant nor impeccable. It can sin both intellectually and morally. It is a sinful body made up of sinful men and women, now gloriously justified through the death and resurrection of Christ on their behalf, but nonetheless still full of spots and wrinkles and many other such things. Paul writes to the New Testament Christians and to others about all manner of doctrinal errors and specific sins which he calls by their nasty names. We must not press this wonderful metaphor of the body to the extent of identifying the glorified body of the God-man in heaven with the fallible and sinful body of the church on earth.

This illustration of the church is one given to us by the Holy Spirit, but we must be careful not to press the analogy to an unwarranted extreme and to draw significant doctrinal conclusions which are not drawn in Scripture. The crucial point which emerges, however, is surely that a congregation is more than an aggregation, that a body is something quite different from a pile of minced meat! A body is organized and the parts function together. The body of Christ in the local congregation is meant to function intimately together like the parts of a body complementing each other, and mutually nourishing and serving each other.

---

[5] See Alan Cole, *The Body of Christ* (Westminster, England: Hodder & Stoughton, 1964), for a helpful treatment of this subject.

[6] See chapter 3, "The sinfulness and fallibility of the church."

In North America recently there has been a most encouraging stress upon what they are calling "body-life."

> Christian meetings have turned into dull-stodgy rituals where many Christians gather to go through completely predictable performances, all conducted in an atmosphere of "reverence" which permits no interchange with one another, no exchange of thought, no discussion of truth, and no opportunity to display Christian love in any but the most superficial of ways.

> What is terribly missing is the experience of "body-life"; that warm fellowship of Christian with Christian which the New Testament calls *koinonia*… In the early church a kind of rhythm of life was evident in which the Christians would gather together in homes to instruct one another, study and pray together, and share the ministry of spiritual gifts. Then they would go out into the world again to let the warmth and glow of their love-filled lives overflow into a spontaneous Christian witness that drew love-starved pagans like a candy store draws little children…

> The present-day church has managed to do away with *koinonia* almost completely, reducing the witness of the church to proclamation (kerygma) alone.

Some Important Lessons for Today

From the theory of the meaning of the illustration, therefore, we turn happily to the wonder of the reality which Ray Stedman describes so vividly in his book. Paul seems to draw five main lessons from the use of this particular illustration.

1. The unity of the body

Paul is disturbed by divisions in the Corinthian church and so writes urging "that all of you agree and that there be no dissensions among you, but that you be united (*katartizō*) in the same mind and in the same judgment" (1 Cor 1:10b). It is significant that he here uses the verb from the same root as the word translated "equipment" of the saints which, as we have already seen, refers to bringing together into correct articulation members who had become separate from each other. Paul goes on, "Is Christ divided?" (1 Cor 1:13a). We all belong to Christ. All true believers are members of his body. It is for this reason that they must be "eager to maintain the unity of the Spirit in the bond of peace. There is one body and one Spirit, just as you were called to the one hope that belongs to your call, one Lord, one faith, one baptism, one God and Father of us all" (Eph 4:3-6a).

This emphasis on the unity of the body is directed against divisiveness and faction. Any congregation or assembly of Christians contains not only a pyramid of ages, but a spectrum of opinions. One of the ways in which a congregation "grows," or enjoys a corporate sanctification, is in learning to function together as one body. There is always a danger of polarization into an exclusive faction of somewhat narrow-minded, rigorist conservatives and a more tolerant faction of open-minded progressives (Rom 14). Equally the generation gap makes the older generation critical of the younger and the younger impatient of the older. This does not mean, however, that either group is permitted, even mentally, to excommunicate the others. However, much I find it difficult to digest their opinions, I have to recognize that others have as much right to belong to the body of Christ as I do, if they are truly joined to Christ. The church is not the group of people chosen by me, but the group chosen by God. They are *his* elect.

I remember having as a child a fantasy gang with whom I played mentally in those final moments before going to sleep. It consisted of all the nicest boys and girls that I knew, and excluded anyone whom I did not appreciate.

> The idea of the invisible church, in its popular use, derives its main attraction—unless I am much mistaken—from the fact that each of us can determine its membership as he will. It is *our* ideal church, containing the people whom we—in our present stage of spiritual development—would regard as fit members… The congregation of God is something quite different. It is the company of people whom it has pleased God to call into the fellowship of his Son. *Its members are chosen by him, not by us, and we have to accept them whether we like them or not.* It is not a segregation but a congregation, and the power by which it is constituted is the divine love which loves even the unlovely and reaches out to save all men.[7]

Paul mentions the foolish individual who says, "I do not belong to the body" (1 Cor 12:15b). This is just nonsense. You cannot be a Christian

---

[7] Newbigin, *The Household of God*, p.29 (italics mine).

without belonging. If you are in Christ, then you are joined to him and through him to all others who are joined to him. Salvation is not my being isolated in a hermetically sealed space capsule, but my being thrown together in community with a lot of other people chosen by God.

It is a community of grace—so that the others, like myself, are chosen, not on a basis of merit because they are "nice people," but because of their need, repentance, and faith. I have to accept that they are as equally chosen and elect as I am myself. (This may be difficult with the lunatic fringe of any congregation!)

Christ's choice of the twelve apostles provides an interesting illustration. The number of the twelve was clearly a matter of choice (Matt 19:28) and it seems clear that not only the number, but the individuals who made up that number were chosen by him: impetuous Peter, the choleric "sons of thunder" James and John, dishonest Judas, cynical Thomas and the rest. Christ did not choose a group who were easy to work with and he may not choose an easy group for us to work with either.

Divisiveness, therefore, is definitely condemned. I must do my utmost to maintain the unity of the Spirit and do nothing that would put myself out of joint with others, still less encourage faction or division in the body. So often we justify a personality clash between strong characters by discovering some doctrinal rationalization for criticizing the other person. We ignore our points of agreement and magnify our differences. We become all too inclined to believe any lie or distorted story that the devil whispers in our ears about those with whom we are at odds. Because we are not communicating with each other, neither of us can check the veracity of the story, and perhaps we don't really want to do so.

In this connection it is significant that, though the Galatian and Corinthian churches were in serious error on cardinal points of doctrine, Paul nowhere suggests that he is going to withdraw or form his own faction into a new, "sound" church. If anything, the reverse. It is not a matter of dividing the church because false doctrine has arisen; rather it is a question of getting rid of false teaching precisely because the church is one. Paul is under no illusions about the possibility of wolves disturbing the flock, or even of some doctrinally woolly sheep giving false teaching (Acts 20:29, 30). Even in a strong passage about the unity of the body Paul warns about the danger of being caused to spin round and round by "every wind of doctrine, by human cunning, by craftiness in deceitful schemes" (Eph 4:14). At the same time, he seems to feel that a congregation under the guidance of the Spirit, given sound biblical teaching, ought to be of one heart and one mind. They ought to be able to recognize the difference between true, primitive, apostolic teaching, what he calls in Ephesians 2:20 "the foundation of the apostles and prophets," and any later theological novelties introduced by false teachers.

I sometimes wonder whether we Evangelicals are not too ready to write off unbiblical people as "liberals," and mentally to excommunicate them, without first of all doing our utmost to reclaim them for the truth. They may be liberals simply because they have never heard an intelligent presentation of a sound biblical faith. If the faith "once for all delivered to the saints" is indeed the truth that sets men free, then we should believe that, through the power of the Holy Spirit, men can be genuinely released from the subtleties of intellectual error as they may be from the allurements of moral sin.

2. The diversity of the members

The fact that the members of the body all have different contributions to make is a commonplace, but it is so stressed in the various body passages that we need to take a fresh look at its importance, and all the more because many Christians fail to grasp its implications. "But grace was given to each one of us according to the measure of Christ's gift," writes Paul in Ephesians 4:7, and it is extremely significant that in a corporate passage of this nature there should be this insistence on our each being given grace for the benefit of the whole body. We find the same thought in 1 Corinthians 12:7: "To each is given the manifestation of the Spirit for the common good," and again in 1 Peter 4:10: "As each has received a gift, use it to serve one another, as good stewards of God's varied grace." Each of us as a member of the body has some particular part to play. Paul reminds us of this in Romans 12:4-6 and goes on to list as examples of what he has in mind: those who exercise the gifts of prophecy, of service, of teaching, of exhorting, of giving, of giving aid, and of showing mercy.

Paul would have little use for the "one-man band" type of church which we so often see today. In an orchestra, the task of the conductor is to get all the players functioning together and playing in harmony. It is not his job to dash madly around the seats playing all the instruments himself one after another! To behave in this way is a denial of the diversity of gifts and the sharing of those gifts among all the members of the congregation.

The pattern of diversity is developed in detail in 1 Corinthians 12, in which we are told that there are varieties of gifts, ministries, and workings. This subject has recently been treated at length in another book and I have no wish to go over the same ground.[8] But let me just underline what I have already said: the principle of diversity cannot possibly be distorted to mean that every member of the body is intended to exercise any one particular gift, even the gift of tongues. 1 Corinthians 14 must always be so expounded that it does not contradict the pattern of diversity of members and functions expressed in chapter 12.

3. God's sovereignty over the body

The church is the body of Christ: it is *his* body. "For in one Spirit we were all baptized into one body" (1 Cor 12:13); and most significantly, "All these (*i.e.* the various gifts) are empowered by one and the same Spirit, who apportions to each one individually *as he wills*" (1 Cor 12:11, emphasis added). The sovereignty of God the Holy Spirit in giving the gifts and characteristic functions to each individual is clear.

We may seek gifts, but we may not demand them.

As suggested earlier,[9] the plural nature of this passage is such that "you" does not mean that an individual should seek gifts for himself alone. Rather, we have a plural, "yous," meaning that the congregation is to seek gifts for itself, praying that the Holy Spirit will give to certain individuals of its number all the specific, helpful gifts required for the growth and building up of the congregation.

Paul then develops the body analogy in great detail—feet, hands, ears, eyes, the head, and less honorable members are all mentioned. Finally, there comes a further list of diverse gifts, and the strongly rhetorical questions demanding the answer "No" in the grammatical form in which they are cast, beginning with what we could translate as, "All are not apostles, are they?"; and so on.

We need to accept this from God. He instructs us in the part we are to play in the body of which Christ is the head. One meets Christians who are envious of others, or who waste years wishing they were different, and that they had the gifts of somebody else. One meets shy men and women

---

[8] See Donald Bridge and David Phypers, *Spiritual Gifts and the Church* (Downers Grove, Illinois: InterVarsity Press, 1973).

[9] See Chapter 2- "Salvation More Than Personal," under the subheading "Confusions of English Grammar."

who wish that they were extroverts. But God made shy men and women, and chose shy men and women, because he wants other shy men and women brought to faith, and they might well be put off by the cheerful extrovert with his powerful presentation and glib explanations. God's sovereignty extends to the kind of people we are by disposition and we need to give this back to him for him to perfect. A congregation made up entirely of strong, natural leaders with the gift of preaching would be devastating! Four and twenty blackbirds all beginning to sing at once would be nothing to this!

A diversity of gifts among the members, then, is God's sovereign provision for a congregation. We have to accept that not only may it be his sovereign pleasure to give a particular gift to me but it is also his sovereign right to refuse it to me. By its very nature a gift is something which cannot be deserved and cannot be demanded.

4. Interdependence

This is the very opposite of individualism. "God has so composed the body... that the members may have the same care for one another. If one member suffers, all suffer together; if one member is honored, all rejoice together" (1 Cor 12:24b, 25b, 26). I have to recognize my need of others and their need of me. I cannot be like that foolish member of the body which says to other members, "I have no need of you" (1 Cor 12:21a). I am not a self-sufficient unit. I belong to other Christians and I need those other Christians. Eyes and ears are superb pieces of physiological engineering, and technically fantastic; but they are quite useless on their own. They need a head and a neck to turn them in various directions and legs to carry them around. They require hands to act upon what they see and hear.

Many people give lip service to this principle but are still impoverished by their individualism. There are those sad and badly instructed people who want to exercise a ministry, perhaps in some interdenominational group, but who merely "attend" a local church, or go around sermon-tasting in a number of different evangelical churches and who are thus badly adrift from their biblical moorings. The whole emphasis of Scripture is that Christians *need* the body, need each other, and cannot really exist as healthy, balanced Christians except as members of the body. To be "an independent operator," a kind of free-lance Christian, is not only to be missing the blessing you should derive from others, but also to be depriving them of your own contribution. It is not enough to say that you are a member of the universal church. You are properly required to be a member of that church "in local circumscription."

The spectator Christian who merely attends services is missing part of the gospel. He is a Christian in so far as his relationship to God is concerned, but not in his relationship to fellow Christians. His whole view of the gospel and the church is deficient. He not only needs to sit under the ministry of the gifted pastor-teacher; he also needs the proper relationship with other members of the body. As we have already seen, the metaphor of the body is interestingly developed by Paul in Ephesians 4:11-16 where he speaks of the function of the apostles, prophets, evangelists, and pastor-teachers as being "to equip God's people for work in his service, to the building up of the body of Christ" (Eph 4:12, NEB).[10]

It is worth a brief paragraph enlarging on what we have already said about *katartismos* and *katartizō*, which carry the force of rendering something *artios*—of making it capable or useful, to enable it to perform the function for which it was made, or "to make one what one ought to be." This is well illustrated from the occasion when the sons of Zebedee were "mending" their nets (Matt 4:21). This is again the same word. The fishermen were getting their nets ready so that they could exercise their proper function. Dirty, torn, and tangled nets would be useless. So, James and John cleaned off the seaweed, mended the holes, and folded the nets ready for use. The work of the specially gifted ministers (Eph 4:11) is to equip or prepare the congregation so that they fulfilll their function. If the new of the congregation is all fouled up, full of rents, and thoroughly disorganized, it will be quite ineffective for catching men as spiritual fish. The saints must be properly knit together, functioning together efficiently if they are to welcome and bring in newcomers properly.

We have already mentioned Galen, the Greek physician, who uses this word of reducing fractures and dislocations.[11] The same word occurs again in Galatians 6:1, "Brothers, if anyone is caught in any transgression, you who are spiritual should restore (*i.e. 'mend')* him," that is, bring that member back into proper articulation with all the other members.

---

[10] Please note that the commas in the AV and RSV are positively misleading. The AV suggests that the work of the special ministers is the threefold task of 1) equipping the saints, 2) the work of the ministry, and 3) building up the body of Christ. The RSV suggests that their work is twofold: 1) equipping the saints for the work of ministry, and 2) building up the body of Christ. There are no commas in the Greek text and the force of the passage in its own context and in that of the whole New Testament is that the body is built up when the saints are exercising the work of the ministry as a result of the work of the special ministers.

[11] As referred to earlier in this chapter.

We do have a remarkable influence upon one another. If one member backslides, all are influenced for the worse. If one is blessed, then all are influenced for good. Some of us have probably appreciated how our ability to fulfilll our functions can be seriously impaired when just one thing goes wrong with our car. The whole engine doesn't have to fall out before the car stops. Similarly, one doesn't have to have heart failure or a brain hemorrhage before the body begins to suffer. A comparatively small hole in a tooth, or septic area on the limb, or a suppurating appendix, can affect the whole body. The body doesn't have to be all wrong before it begins to suffer.

In the same way, we need to recognize that the principle of mutuality works in both directions. My failure is not just my own business; others are going to be affected by me. It is possible for us to think very selfishly about our salvation and to feel that our own personal behavior is entirely our own affair. The principle of mutuality reminds us that, whether we like it or not, we affect one another within the body both for good and ill.

All of us need the ministry of others to help us. We mustn't resent it, grudge it, or resist it, but rather accept it gladly and rejoice. My wife and I returned to the Far East after a furlough in Britain as members of a local church praising God for all that the ministry of others had meant to us, not only in what one might regard as "spiritual matters," but also in essentially practical ones—the lady who took our infant off our hands so that we could pack, for example, and her husband who helped us with some final chores.

All of us need to minister to others. The biblical command to love our neighbors has to find some outlet and to be shown somehow. So often we do not appreciate our need of the ministry of others and our responsibility to minister to them until some crisis such as sickness or death gives the opportunity to show and to receive love. But this is to miss the force of Paul's references in Ephesians 4:16 and Colossians 2:19 to the way in which the body is made up of joints, ligaments, sinews, and the like. Unless these are functioning all the time and working properly, bodily growth will never take place. The very fact that we are part of the body means that we have something to contribute to it.

All of us need others to help us understand the truth of God's Word. In Bible study, we begin to understand "with all saints" things which we would not have discovered on our own. Even when a Christian claims to be speaking under the direct inspiration of the Holy Spirit, Scripture provides that the others must weigh what is said (1 Cor 14:29). We realize that all preaching is a mixed phenomenon. Some of it is clearly given by the Spirit and goes far beyond what we intended to say when we were preparing. Other parts we recognize as very human. There were things we put very badly or which we wished afterwards we had not said. This scriptural provision recognizes that individuals have no monopoly of truth and may, with the best of intentions, pass on their own fallible impressions and ideas in the middle of what otherwise is God-given material. There has to be discussion and debate, so that we modify and correct one another's ideas. Significantly, preaching in the "one-man band" congregation does not allow for this kind of correction. Godly preachers who hear only themselves preach can become isolated and distorted in their emphasis unless they are corrected by sitting under the ministry and teaching of others. There is a real danger of individualism when we are exposed only to our own ideas. We need others to deepen our understanding.

All of us need others in developing the new, beautiful lifestyle. It is significant that the "fruit of the Spirit" (Gal 5:22, 23) is not on the whole something to be experienced on one's own. Love, patience, kindness, generosity, gentleness, and self-control all demand the presence of at least one other human being. Solitary sainthood is unknown to the New Testament. It is when two or three saints are put together that problems begin to develop! We sometimes help each other because we are difficult to live with and quite unintentionally, therefore, we sanctify one another! Richard Baxter in his *Christian Directory* speaks of the wife's being a chief instrument in her husband's sanctification and of her husband's being a chief instrument in his wife's sanctification! Both the difficulties and the resultant blessings are mutual. So it is with the new Christian community.

5. The maturity of the body

The final significant element is Paul's teaching about the body is growth and development. This theme is especially marked in Ephesians, that general Letter applicable to any congregation. In chapter 4, Paul writes of God's gifts to the church, made in order "to equip God's people for work in his service, to the building up of the body of Christ" (Eph 4:12, NEB). He then continues:

> ... until we all attain to the unity of the faith and of the
> knowledge of the Son of God, to mature manhood, to the
> measure of the stature of the fullness of Christ... we are to
> grow up in every way into him who is the head, into Christ,

from whom the whole body, joined and held together by
every joint with which it is equipped, when each part is working properly, makes the *body grow* so that it *builds* itself up in
love (Eph 4:13, 15, 16, emphasis added).

There is a tremendous piling up of ideas here—growth, full maturity,
development to full adult stature, and so on. It is not enough that the
congregation exists: it must grow and develop and make progress. I
remember once asking a group of Batak elders in Sumatra, "What are
you praying that the Lord will do for you?" I still remember the puzzled
expression on their faces and the frank reply: "We have never thought
about it." And lest we should think ourselves to be superior, let us ask
ourselves how many congregations do have real prayer goals in this way?
So often, provided the building is kept in good repair and the seats
reasonably full, that is regarded as an adequate measure of success. Our
prayers should, of course, include evangelistic goals. The congregation
should grow and multiply in this sense and spawn off new daughter
congregations. But world evangelization is not the supreme end of the
church. It is only a means towards that end. We need to be praying for
a perfecting of the congregation as a community developing a beautiful
lifestyle in the midst of a corrupt and disintegrating world order.

In Ephesians 4:12, the phrase "to equip (literally, 'for the equipment
of') the saints" is translated in the AV as "perfecting the saints." We can
enlarge on this meaning by introducing the athletic concept of "bringing
into perfect condition." Paul uses the related verb (*katartizō*) in concluding his second Letter to the Corinthians when he prays "that you be made
complete," and goes on to exhort them to "be made complete" (2 Cor
13:9, 11, NASB). Just as human bodies vary tremendously in their development, so also do congregations. There is the body on the dissecting slab
in the university anatomy department, dismembered, with bits hanging
off in all directions: unfortunately, a fair picture of some congregations
one meets! Then there is the flabby, sluggish, out of condition body which
is not being exercised. There is also the body of the athlete brought to peak
condition for the Olympic games, perfectly coordinated and disciplined
with magnificent muscle tone, beautifully poised for the supreme effort.
This is what the Christian body of the congregation is meant to be like.
This is our goal in the corporate sanctification of the congregation. Just as
we look for the perfecting of the Christian individual, as a new man made
in the likeness of the Lord Jesus, so also we look for the perfecting of the
congregation, as a new community in which all the members are each
making a perfect contribution in relation to all the others. This certainly

adds a new dimension to sanctification! It's not enough that I should be a solitary saint; I have to act in perfect harmony with all the others.

It seems fitting to conclude this chapter as the writer to the Hebrews concluded his Letter, also using the word *katartizō*.

> Now may the God of peace who brought again from the dead our Lord Jesus, the great shepherd of the sheep, by the blood of the eternal covenant, *equip you* with everything good that you may do his will, working in us that which is pleasing in his sight, through Jesus Christ, to whom be glory forever and ever. Amen (Heb 13:20, 21, emphasis added).

Chapter 5 - The Goal of Salvation

That he might present the church to himself in splendor,
without spot or wrinkle or any such thing, that she
might be holy and without blemish. (Eph 5:27)

The majority of congregations encountered today in any part of the world are not goal oriented churches at all. They are, as Stephen Clark points out mainly activity oriented or problem orientated. How true it is that much church life is merely a sum of meetings and activities: Morning Prayer, Evening Prayer, Holy Communion and Mothers Union in one tradition or breaking of bread, plus gospel meeting, plus prayer meeting, plus young people, in a different one. Our sense of a goal for the congregation has been lost, and we tend to think only in terms of activities. Clark reminds us that an architect always keeps his eyes firmly fixed upon the finished product as outlined in the plans. Paul describes himself as a "wise master builder" (in Greek, *architektōn*) and urges us to take care how we build. We cannot be taking much care if we lose sight of our goal through preoccupation with ways and means and with activities which have lost their purpose. When invited to speak at a meeting, the most embarrassing question to ask the organizers is, 'What is the purpose of the meeting?', and it is unusual to be given anything but an evasive reply.

In the introduction to this book we suggested that the church today may be likened to a Cinderella who has forgotten the glorious truth expressed in the verse which heads this chapter. As a result, there often seems to be little concern about the spots and wrinkles which at present undoubtedly exist. Nevertheless, the church is pictured in the New Testament as the

bride of Christ, and the marriage of the Lamb is seen as the great culmi-
nation of all salvation history:

> And I saw the holy city, new Jerusalem, coming down out
> of heaven from God, prepared as a bride adorned for her
> husband… "Come, I will show you the Bride, the wife of the
> Lamb" (Rev 21:2, 9).

The church's goal is to become the beautiful and perfect new society, the
new Utopia brought into existence by God himself. Certainly, she is far
from perfect now, but she will be made perfect and glorious when that
great day comes. Paul is writing to the Philippians in a plural sense when
he says, "He who began a good work in you (*i.e.* the Philippian congregation) will complete it in the day of Jesus Christ, without a doubt, I am
certain."

Old Testament Roots

The Hebrew word *kallāh* used for "bride" means a complete or perfect
one, a woman brought to the full perfection of womanhood and beauty
on her wedding day. Unlike the metaphor of the body, this vivid picture
of the church has very strong Old Testament roots, for the idea of the
Lord as the husband or bridegroom of his people is a common one.

> For as a young man marries a young woman,
> so shall your sons marry you,
> and as the bridegroom rejoices over the bride,
> so shall your God rejoice over you.   (Isa 62:5)

The prophet Hosea is able to illustrate the idea from his own experience
of an unhappy marriage, which he makes an acted prophecy of what the
Lord will do for his faithless people.

> "And in that day, declares the Lord, you will call me 'My
> Husband,'…And I will betroth you to me forever. I will
> betroth you to me in righteousness and in justice, in steadfast
> love and in mercy. I will betroth you to me in faithfulness.
> And you shall know the Lord" (Hos 2:16a, 19, 20).

The prophet Ezekiel most vividly portrays Jerusalem as the unfaithful
wife of the Lord: "I made my vow to you and entered into a covenant
with you, declares the Lord God, and you became mine" (Ezek 16:8b).
The whole passage is worth reading, for it provides a striking illustration
of the Old Testament concept of God's people as being like an unfaithful

wife. In many ways it is a depressing picture; yet we are also shown God's faithfulness and patience towards his repeatedly unfaithful people. In church history, also, we are saddened by doctrinal apostasy and spiritual coldness; the institutional formality of the church's feeble love for Christ at some periods is utterly depressing. But the Old Testament illustration encourages us to believe that, in the final issue, God will fulfill his great and glorious purpose to present the church to himself as a beautiful new community. This Old Testament background was no doubt in our Lord's mind when he described himself as "the bride-groom" and John the Baptist as the bridegroom's friend or 'best man'.

How is the Church to be Perfected?

We have discovered already that the Letter to the Ephesians is full of the most striking group portraits of corporate salvation in the church. In a passage which is primarily about marriage, Paul cannot resist drawing the parallels with the relationship between the loving Christ and the church as his bride.

> For the husband is the head of the wife even as Christ is
> the head of the church, his body, and is himself its Savior.
> Now as the church submits to Christ, so also wives should
> submit in everything to their husbands. Husbands, love your
> wives, as Christ loved the church and gave himself up for
> her, that he might sanctify her, having cleansed her by the
> washing of water with the word, so that he might present
> the church to himself in splendor, without spot or wrinkle or
> any such thing, that she might be holy and without blemish.
> (Eph 5:23-27).

It seems, therefore, that the anticipated perfection of the bride is a moral perfection expressed in a visible holiness. The bride must be beauti-ful and her holiness is a visible and attractive perfection. There are two Greek words used in the New Testament translated as "good." *Agathos* refers to that which is morally and ethically good, while *kalos* means aesthetically and beautifully good. This second word, deriving from the Greek appreciation of physical beauty, is frequently used of "good works" in the New Testament, and reminds us that the church is to be *seen* to be lovely and beautiful. The people of God are to be good to look upon. A mere moral and ethical goodness might appear cold and forbidding. New Testament goodness is to be a gorgeous goodness that delights the eyes. Just as the individual is to grow in holiness, so also the Christian congregation is to grow in warm, generous beauty.

But there is a second idea present in the New Testament—an intellectual or doctrinal growth in knowledge. Thus, Paul writes to the Corinthian congregation which has been causing him such distress:

> I feel a divine jealousy for you, since I betrothed you to one husband, to present you as a pure virgin to Christ. But I am afraid that as the serpent deceived Eve by his cunning, your thoughts will be led astray from a sincere and pure devotion to Christ. For if someone comes and proclaims another Jesus than the one we proclaimed, or if you receive a different spirit from the one you received, or if you accept a different gospel from the one you accepted, you put up with it readily enough (2 Cor 11:2-4).

The purity of the bride envisaged here is a doctrinal one; the church is to be pure in the simplicity of its devotion to Christ, and its unsophisticated and unqualified obedience to his teaching. It is the serpent-like subtlety of Satan which is perpetually endeavoring to defile the church by leading her astray from obedience to the clear teaching of God.

Here, then, are the two main areas in which congregations are to be perfected. We are to "grow in the grace and knowledge of our Lord and Savior Jesus Christ" (2 Pet 3:18). Not only as individuals, but also corporately as congregations are we to grow towards perfection morally and intellectually, in behavior and in belief.

The Invisible Bride

Christians from the earliest times have had to wrestle with the problem of impurity in the church. If the church cannot be destroyed by persecution from without, then the devil will always try to spoil things from within. Christ indicated this very clearly when telling the parable of the wheat and the tares, depicting false believers sown among the true.

In Acts (4:32-5:11) we read how Barnabas displayed a truly sacrificial spirit in selling his piece of land and presenting the proceeds to the church. Ananias and Sapphira, however, were prepared to settle for the appearance of dedication rather than the reality of it, and thus were trying to deceive the congregation. The impurity was radically and drastically rooted out. Later Paul talks of impurity in the church as being like yeast which rapidly disseminates itself throughout the whole lump

(1 Cor 5:6-8). The individual who continues in sin is to be publicly disciplined, but the problem still remains. Some congregations do exercise a real discipline on members who persist in willful and flagrant sin. But there are lower levels of inconsistency which may not be dealt with in this way, for all of us are conscious of being inconsistent in some areas and are therefore generally ready both to forbear and to forgive. There is the further problem in less closely-knit congregations of fringe members and nominal Christians where there may be doubts about the validity of their Christian experience and the reality of their Christian behavior.

Church history is full of divisions and attempts to eliminate from the church both impure living and false teaching. The aim has been to separate off a "pure church" which approximates more nearly to the "invisible church" of true believers, thus attempting to make the "visible congregation" as near as possibly coterminous with the "invisible church."

> Since Augustine, but especially since the time of Zwingli and Calvin, with the growing realization of the discrepancy between the New Testament *ecclesia* and the historical 'church,' quite useless attempts have been made to elucidate the relationship between two quantities by drawing a distinction between a visible and invisible church…This desperate expedient has been vainly used in the attempt to explain the disparity between the actual churchly institution and the New Testament idea of the *ecclesia*. But these twin conceptions, so far from clarifying what was intended, have served but to increase the confusion…The New Testament *ecclesia*, the fellowship of Jesus Christ, is a pure communion of persons and has nothing of the character of an institution about it: it is therefore misleading to identify any single one of the historically developed churches, which are all marked by an institutional character, with the true Christian communion.[1]

No doubt we are familiar with this tendency to a polarization between the larger, "comprehensive" churches on the one hand, made up of a mixed multitude of genuine believers and nominal Christians, and separatist, independent congregations on the other hand, with a clear line demarcating their membership and a determination to maintain some degree of purity of belief and occasionally of behavior as well! The choice facing us is not between a visible church of which we are ashamed and an invisible church of which we would be justly proud if only we could see it, but rather between two different kinds of visible church. Both

---

[1] Brunner, *The Misunderstanding of the Church*, p.17.

poorly worded. How could you tell the difference?

56   MISSIONAL BODY: THE BEAUTY AND PURPOSE OF THE CHURCH

consist of wheat and tares in varying proportions. While the one makes little attempt to deal with the tares, the other endeavors to do its own weeding, but finds it difficult to distinguish between some rather inconsistent wheat and some particularly convincing tares! As fallible human beings, we find it difficult to distinguish between true and false professions. While there are always those about whom we may feel reasonably certain, there are nevertheless a considerable number in the visible congregation who appear to be hybrids.

Read 1 Corinthians 1:2-9 and notice the language Paul uses in addressing the congregation at Corinth. They are "sanctified in Christ Jesus;" in every way they have been "enriched in him with all speech and all knowledge", they are "not lacking in any gift." It seems remarkable that Paul can write in this way about a visible congregation, especially as it emerges from the rest of the Letter that he was under no illusions about either their moral or their doctrinal impurity and faithlessness. Later he calls them "carnal," and toward the conclusion of his second Letter urges them to examine themselves to see whether they are holding to their faith (see 2 Cor 13:5).

Paul never seems to take refuge and comfort in the concept of a pure "invisible" church. Instead, he deals practically with the visible congregation as it is. We too must face the fact that what we have to grapple with is a visible community. There seems little point in belonging to an invisible congregation made up of invisible men! We are not concerned with an invisible bride. We are concerned with an exceedingly visible and fallible Cinderella who has all but forgotten that she is looking forward to a future "royal wedding" with the King of kings.

Is Church Membership Biblical?

This would seem the point at which to raise the important issue of whether the concept of church membership is a biblical one or not. It would certainly be possible from the New Testament to make out a case that the only kind of church membership known to the New Testament is membership of the church universal through becoming incorporated "in Christ." Through repentance and faith, outwardly witnessed in Christian baptism, an individual became a member of the church universal and thereafter, it would appear, was automatically accepted on that basis as a member of the local congregation of Christians in the place where he lived. In the first century, Christians such as Aquila and Priscilla seem to have moved around the Mediterranean world and to have been successfully members of the churches at Corinth, Ephesus, and Rome. The whole concept of "transfer of membership" from one local congregation to another would seem foreign to the New Testament. There was, however, the most excellent practice of writing letters of commendation; Paul on varying occasions commends Timothy (1 Cor 16:10f.), Titus (2 Cor 8:23f.), Phoebe (Rom 16:1f.) and Mark (Col 4:10). When Apollos had been more excellently instructed in the way by Priscilla and Aquila, the brethren in Ephesus encouraged him to go on to Achaia and "wrote to the disciples to receive him" (Acts 18:27). Certainly in missionary situations, if this excellent practice was always followed, we should be delivered from many trouble makers, frauds, and hypocrites!

There was a time when I would have maintained strongly that the whole concept of church membership in a local congregation was unscriptural. There may indeed be good arguments against church membership as a form of human organization, but the necessity of really belonging to a local congregation of Christians and accepting both responsibility and discipline is surely crucial to a proper biblical understanding of the doctrine of the church. There is nothing necessarily unspiritual about a roll of members, for Christ told his disciples to "rejoice that your names are written in heaven" (Luke 10:20b) and the assembly of the firstborn "are enrolled in heaven" (Heb 12:23). Certainly there appears to have been some kind of roll of widows (1 Tim 5:9, 11) and the statistics given in Acts would seem to indicate that the newly Spirit-filled congregation did not consider it unspiritual to number its membership.

This ought not to be decided by purely theoretical considerations. The following practical reasons for being clear about actually belonging to a congregation would seem admissible:

1. People ought not to be allowed to drift in and out of congregations as mere spectators. We must insist that individuals accept responsibility towards, and involvement in, a local congregation.

2. We all need to be answerable to Christian elders who will watch over our souls (Heb 13:17). There is real blessing in having older Christians who feel a responsibility for us and who are prepared to speak to us frankly. As leader of a large missionary society I have seen the blessing arising from the fact that all our members are responsible to somebody else, and someone feels responsible for their pastoral oversight. It is good to know also that there is someone to whom you can go for spiritual help. I rejoice that

my membership of a local congregation is not just a theoretical consideration, but that there are people who feel responsible for me and to whom I feel responsible.

3. If membership of the congregation is to be meaningful, then its members must have opportunity to say what they think about the life and conduct of the community in all its worship and activities. It is important, therefore, to distinguish between casual visitors and local members who feel that they belong to, and wish to play a responsible part in, the congregation.

4. If there is no concept of membership and responsibility, it is very difficult to exercise discipline over those who make up the congregation in order to help them to put right things that are wrong. If someone who is disciplined in one congregation can merely drift out of it and into another, such discipline becomes pointless.

The Moral Purity of the Bride

A reader of Ephesians 4 finds himself asking, "What in fact does it mean 'to walk in a manner worthy of the calling to which you have been called' (v.1b)? And what does it mean to 'grow up in every way into him who is the head' (v.15b)?" Paul first defines it negatively as, "you must no longer walk as the Gentiles do" (v.17b). He is not content, however, to set it out in purely negative terms. It is not enough to put away false-hood, but everyone must speak the truth with his neighbor, for "we are members one of another" (v.25b). It is not enough merely to refrain from stealing, but rather "let him labor, doing honest work with his own hands, so that he may have something to share with anyone in need" (v.28b). It is not enough merely to refrain from "corrupting talk", but we must aim at speech which will edify and "give grace to those who hear" (v.29b). And not only must we abstain from "crude joking" (*eutrapelia*) about sex but rather our attitude is to be a positive one of thanksgiving (*eucharistia*) (5:4; note that Paul is also engaging in a little word play!).

It is important to realize that the life of the Christian community is not merely a negative abstention from vice, but a positive display of Christian virtue. Paul express this very vividly in the same passage when he says, "Fling off the dirty clothes of the old way of living...and...put on the clean fresh clothes of the new life."[2] There is a kind of Christian negative

---

[2] J. B. Phillips' translation of Eph 4:22, 24.

holiness which rejoices in discarding various forms of worldliness, but which leaves the individual stark naked. True Christian holiness demands also the putting on of the positive virtues like a suit of beautiful new clothes.

The new community must be marked by a new lifestyle.

In Acts 20:31 Paul describes his remarkable ministry to the Ephesians in terms of a ministry of admonishing, which would appear to be almost a lost dimension of teaching in our day. Even allowing for preacher's license and hyperbole, it indicates a form of corrective ministry designed to ensure that the lifestyle of the new community was pleasing to God. Writing to the Colossians, Paul indicates that this is not merely his apostolic responsibility (1:28), but a responsibility which all Christians have to all others. "Let the word of Christ dwell in you richly," he says; "teaching and admonishing one another in all wisdom" (3:16). To be frank, our congregational life has degenerated to such an extent that this kind of rich fellowship where "admonishing" can take place is remarkably rare. If it happens at all, most of us feel so embarrassed that we have to screw up our courage to say anything critical of another, being only to conscious of our own personal inconsistencies. We are so ready to take offense, and so careful of not giving it, that sometimes our fellowship can only be described as Lucy described Charlie Brown—'wishy-washy'. To our modern way of thinking, admonishing others seems somewhat priggish.

Because of our extreme individualism, we tend to feel that our inconsistencies in Christian behavior are an entirely private and personal affair. 'Mind your own business!' is the individualistic rejoinder, barely stifled by our feeling that this would be an unspiritual reply! But if the whole church is going to be affected and defiled by my inconsistencies, if this is leaven which will defile the whole congregational lump, then I need to begin to ask myself whether my inconsistencies and sins are such a private affair as I imagine. None of us is sinless, but where congregational fellowship is rich and deep and real, we shall be ready to seek to help one another to flee temptation and achieve obedience.

At the earlier Methodist class meetings, members were expected every week to answer some extremely personal questions such as the following: Have you experienced any particular temptations during the past week? How did you react or respond to those temptations? Is there anything you are trying to keep secret, and if so, why? At this point the modern Christian swallows hard! We are often coated with a thick layer of reserve and modesty which covers "a multitude of sins;" usually our own. Significantly James 5:16-20, the original context of that phrase, is the passage which urges, "Confess your sins to one another, and pray for one another, that you may be healed." James also reminds us of the prayer of Elijah, "a man with a nature like ours," and goes on to talk about bringing back a sinner from the error of his way, thus saving his soul from death and covering a multitude of sins. The same openness and readiness to confess to one another and pray for one another as fellow sinners is manifest here too.

The Doctrinal Purity of the Bride

If God has revealed truth about himself in the great, cardinal doctrines of the deity of Christ, his objective, finished work on Calvary, and his real resurrection in the body, then to forsake these revealed truths for inadequate human guesswork is spiritual adultery. But lest we pat ourselves upon our evangelical backs and admire ourselves in the mirror for our straight orthodoxy, let us face the fact that all Christians in this world are in various respects and in varying degrees defective both in their understanding of biblical doctrines and in their enjoyment of biblical blessings. "For we know in part and we prophesy in part... now we see in a mirror dimly, but then face to face. Now I know in part; then I shall know fully, even as I have been fully known" (1 Cor 13:9, 12). Each of us has to be encouraged to grow in our doctrinal understanding and knowledge of God's revealed truth, and also in our true experience of the doctrines which we intellectually understand. Having said that, however, what do we do when we are involved in a situation where an individual or a group is denying a cardinal doctrine of the historic Christian faith? This surely is not the situation Paul had in mind when he urged the Ephesians to "maintain the unity of the Spirit in the bond of peace". Here he was thinking of those matters of comparative indifference on which Christians equally loyal to the teaching of the Word of God may at times disagree. He himself had strong views about Christian liberty over the observation of special days and abstention from certain food (Col 2:16, 20ff.), and on occasions would stand very firmly on matters of principle related to them (Gal 2:11f.). Nevertheless, he taught respect for the scruples of others in precisely these areas (Rom 14) and would go out of his way to avoid offending others in matters which he regarded as being of comparative indifference. But when the foundations of the gospel were threatened he would vigorously "contend for the faith that was once for all delivered to the saints" (Jude 3b).

The answer, then, is not that we should opt for one approach to controversy or the other, but that we should always do both. And that would seem to be biblical whether we are in a larger "comprehensive" church or in a smaller, separate, free church.

Let me conclude with a stirring passage from Francis Schaeffer on this subject:

> We must ask, "Do I fight merely for doctrinal faithfulness?" This is like the wife who never sleeps with anybody else, but never shows love to her own husband. Is that a sufficient relationship in marriage? No, ten thousand times, no. Yet if I am a Christian who speaks and acts for doctrinal faithfulness but do not show love to my divine bridegroom, I am in the same place as such a wife. What God wants from us is not only doctrinal faithfulness, but our love day by day. Not in theory, mind you, but in practice.
>
> Those of us who are children of God must realize the seriousness of modern apostasy; we must urge each other not to have any part of it. But at the same time we must be the loving, true bride of the divine bridegroom in reality and in practice, day by day, in the midst of the spiritual adultery of our day. Our call is first to be the bride faithful, but that is not the total call. The call is not only to be the bride faithful, but also to be the bride in love.[3]

And that seems an excellent point at which to turn to a consideration of the church and the family.

---

[3] Francis Schaeffer, *The Church Before the Watching World* (Downers Grove, Illinois: InterVarsity Press, 1972), p. 51.

Chapter 6 – The Church as a family Community

…members of the household of God… (Eph 2:19b)

The dawning consciousness of the newly born infant becomes aware of affectionate faces making doting, drooling noises above its cot. As weeks go by, it learns to recognize first its mother, then its father, and then by gradual degrees its own siblings; the brothers and sisters who share the same home environment. As time passes there will be added further circles of relatives, then family friends, neighborhood children and so on. The child thus grows up as a human being within a world of personal relationships. Modern man has become increasingly aware that a happy environment is just as important for the healthy development of the individual as its hereditary disposition.

We know of the problems which can afflict even adults who have been isolated for long periods in solitary confinement or on a desert island. We may imagine the even more serious consequences if the human infant were brought up entirely in a laboratory incubator maintained at a steady temperature, fed with a balanced diet at regular intervals, and yet isolated entirely from all human encounter and communication. Such a child would have no concept of love and affection. It would hear no human voice whose sounds it might imitate, and thus develop no spoken language of communication. It would not even know those facial grimaces and manual signals which we use to communicate with each other— smiling, laughing, scowling, holding hands, waving goodbye and so on. An intelligent individual might still learn something from its environment, but there would be no teaching and no discipline. The child, even if physically perfect and properly nourished, would yet be desperately impoverished and retarded, both mentally and socially. Recent experiments with monkeys have shown the devastating effects of introducing a hitherto isolated individual of this kind into normal, healthy, simian society. The unfortunate creature is terrified, shows extreme shyness and timidity, cowering away in a corner and developing extreme symptoms of withdrawal.

Spiritual Isolationism

It is alarming to discover similar symptoms in ourselves and other "trousered apes"[1] cowering in spiritual isolation in the back pews of the local church! We have remarked up on the extreme individualism and failure to understand the doctrine of the church that results from our neglect of the Bible's emphasis upon the corporate aspects of salvation. There is even that monstrosity, the drive-in church, which appears to be thoroughly contemporary, related to drive-in banks, drive-in cinemas and the rest, and yet is surely a total denial of what the church is all about. You can go and worship without ever getting out of your car. You don't have to meet anybody! Ugh! Yes, the whole concept of a drive-in church is positively nauseating. But the tragedy is that some church members sitting in pews may be as much walled in by their reserve as they would be by car windows.

Just as we may speak of mental defectives, or of other people as mentally retarded or socially maladjusted, so we might speak of some Christians, genuinely born again and to a certain extent spiritually nourished through their own feeding upon the Word of God, as spiritual defectives who are spiritually retarded and congregationally maladjusted. People who merely maintain their private devotions and who float casually from church to chapel to assembly and back again, grazing and nibbling where their fancy takes them, without becoming properly integrated into and involved in a congregation of God's people, are missing something really essential. They will never develop and mature properly as Christians any more than the child or the monkey reared in isolation in laboratory conditions will develop properly. They are missing out on essential areas of communication and relationship with their fellow believers. They are to be pitied, but they must also be helped.

The problem of reintegrating or reorientating autistic or socially retarded monkeys is apparently a very difficult one. They can sometimes be helped, one gathers, by making them the big monkey in a group of much younger, very immature monkeys. Perhaps this is the principle

---

[1] Publisher's note: This humorous statement should not be taken to mean that human beings are merely apes rather than the image of God.

upon which some Sunday school teachers are appointed! Is this why hitherto reserved and retarded Christian students suddenly blossom when
they are asked to work in beach missions and teenagers' camps? The congregationally maladjusted Christian needs, first of all, to be persuaded
that his isolated individualism is biblically wrong and spiritually deficient.
He must be coaxed out of his cowardice and pathological reserve and
encouraged more and more to enjoy normal human relationships with
his fellow Christians.[2]

It is not enough to use the phrase "born again" and then behave as
though we have been born as orphans in the wilderness. We must recognize that if God has begotten us again, then we have been born into the
new family, the new household of God.

There is no future for the Christian individual in isolation from the
church. The general and proper pattern of the normal Christian life is
to be lived in warm and joyous fellowship with other believers in God's
family. There is a difference between being frozen together and being
melted together, and in a multitude of congregations 'God's frozen people'
need to get warmed up.

There is surely a need for a personal counselling ministry to congregationally maladjusted church members. They are spiritually autistic and
need help to relate to their fellow Christians in a warm fellowship. I do
not want to oversimplify things, but I seriously wonder whether a high
percentage of problems about which Christians seek counseling would
ever arise at all if they had been properly instructed congregationally and
fully integrated into the warm fellowship of God's people.

Spiritual intimacy

When meeting Christians in foreign countries, I always take particular
delight in the verse, "So then you are no longer strangers and aliens, but
you are fellow citizens with the saints and members of the household
of God" (Eph 2:19). This phrase "household of God," and the similar
expression "household of faith" in Galatians 6:10, are a real picture of the

---

[2] Certainly there is a proper reserve and a true spiritual discretion. I am not advocating, for
example, that people should go around openly confessing their most shameful sins to all
and sundry. Sins committed in thought should be confessed in thought to the Lord. Sins
committed by word against other individuals may certainly be confessed in word to those same
individuals in true Christian apology and repentance. Where sins have been committed in act
not only apology but restitution may be necessary. What I am trying to say is that there is a
kind of reserve which results from spiritual retardation in the corporate realm, i.e. what I am
here calling "congregational maladjustment."

intimacy of the family in its warmth and security. This is what the congregation ought to mean to us—a place where we feel safe, can be ourselves, and have no need to be boarded up behind a façade, a place where we are cared for and care for one another. Many other New Testament expressions also imply the intimacy of the family, but some of them have become such clichés that we overlook their warmth and intimacy. We have only to recall such phrases as "bringing many sons to glory" (Heb 2:10b), "he is not ashamed to call them brothers" (Heb 2:11b), "I will tell of your name to my brothers; in the midst of the congregation I will sing your praise" (Heb 2:12), "Behold, I and the children God has given me" (Heb 2:13b), to realize that, although the words are there and the teaching is there, we so often evacuate them of the vibrant warmth of their true meaning.

The congregation is the family of God. We are meant to be able to relax, take our shoes off and let our hair down. Yet so often we dress up and feel very stiff and formal in church, and some even feel that it is only proper and reverent for it to be so! We have made 'going to church' more like a public occasion with pomp and circumstance instead of a family gathering. The family meets to feast and have fun, to relax and to open their hearts to each other. Even the Lord's Supper has tended to degenerate into a formal ceremonial and lost its quality of being a family feast. We may have businessmen's banquets and missionary breakfasts, but oh that there were more opportunity for Christians to eat and drink together before the Lord as a congregation!

A small Japanese congregation at Koganei on the outskirts of Tokyo delighted us in this regard. The congregation had studied the Bible together in all-age Sunday school groups and then met together as a congregation for worship and exposition of the Word of God. Afterwards the chairs were rearranged and we feasted on cheap jam buns or instant noodles. During lunch we talked with each other and usually somebody would be asked to tell us of ways in which the Lord had blessed them recently. Or some member who had attended a Christian conference would be invited to share with the rest of us the blessings enjoyed and lessons learned. Often, we then split up again into different age groups for sharing and discussion of the practical difficulties and problems being encountered in daily living as Christians. Here truly was the congregation meeting as the "household of God," a new, substitute "extended family" to which we were delighted to belong. Certainly, Asian Christians think corporately more easily than do individualistic Westerners. But the Bible is an Asian book and this expectation of a corporate Christian life is clearly delineated for us in the New Testament.

The Church and the Christian Home

A question which will have occurred to you already is, "*How* are we going to realize the goal of making the congregation into an effective community?" Many of us already find our programs are over-extended, and the thought of increasing the congregation's weekly program still further in order to increase everybody's involvement raises immediate questions. Is it at all practicable to increase the number of congregational meetings which Christians might reasonably be expected to attend in the course of a week? In some cases, young married couples who are actively involved in the church see too little of each other as it is, attending meetings on alternate nights while their partner watches over the baby. In commuting areas week-night meetings are already difficult. Existing prayer meetings and other mid-week meetings are often poorly attended in terms of the total Sunday congregation. It seems doubtful, therefore, whether we can expect to increase the *time* spent in meeting together as a congregation, though more small-group activity might be feasible. We could always improve the quality of our meetings. But would that alone deepen the sense of community?

The question arises, where is the new community when it is not meeting together? Does the congregation exist only when it is in plenary session, and is it therefore dissolved between meetings? Or does it exist in a state of suspended animation, kept in cold storage from Monday to Saturday?

The answer to this question is very important.

It provides, incidentally, an interesting illustration of the tendency of Christians to divide their lives into compartmented areas, and even to divide their Bibles into appropriate paragraphs to match! There is a fascinating example of this in Ephesians 5, where many of our Bible versions insert a new paragraph division right in the middle of a Pauline sentence.

The famous exhortation, "Be filled with the Spirit" (Eph 5:18), is not an appeal to the individual to enter upon some second-stage experience, but is, in the context, a continuous plural imperative: "All of you, go on being filled with the Spirit." The comparison is not between and individual dipsomaniac and the individual intoxicated by God's Spirit, but an encouragement to Christians not to spend their limited free time meeting with others in a drunken party or "symposium," but rather to grab every opportunity to meet with other Christians in the congregation. The meaning of being filled with the Spirit is determined in the context by the qualifying participles dependent upon the main verb "be filled".[3] The congregation which is filled by the Holy Spirit will evidence this by "addressing one another", by "singing and making melody", by "giving thanks", and by being subject to one another (Eph 5:19-21). In context, then, this passage would seem to have little to do immediately with an individual entering upon a new level of Christian experience, but a great deal to do with Christian worship and life together in the congregation. How much we all need the help of the Holy Spirit in manifesting true spiritual worship together in the congregation. He will inspire all our speaking (his inspiration is not limited to ecstatic or unintelligible utterance), and all our singing and giving thanks. The whole congregation is to go on repeatedly being filled by the Holy Spirit for all their congregational gatherings that they may truly give glory to God.

The sentence continues by reminding us that another mark of the fullness of the Spirit in the congregation is that its members will "be submitting to one another out of reverence for Christ." Many English versions of the Bible conclude a paragraph at this point and then start a new one beginning, "Wives, submit to your own husbands…" (Eph 5:21f.). The paragraph about church life appears to be concluded; we draw a line across the page and start to talk about something which we place in an entirely separate compartment, namely, family life. Some versions, however, print the words "be submitting" in italics, showing that they have been supplied because they are absent in the original. The drawers of paragraphs have in fact interrupted one of Paul's characteristic long sentences. The Greek original reads, "Be filled with the Spirit…being subject to one another… wives to your husbands as to the Lord," etc. The attitude of wives to their husbands is cited as a particular instance of the general "being subject" to one another incumbent upon all members of the congregation. It is to be manifested by wives to their husbands, by children to their parents and by servants to their employers. The relationships which are singled out here are still part of the one sentence about church life. Family life is not a separate compartment from church life, but an intrinsic part of it. The church continues to be the church, not only when it is actually meeting in congregational session, but also when it meets in smaller groups, as it lives together in Christian families, and as its members, who are "the light of the world" (Matt 5:14a), are scattered throughout society during the

---

[3] See J. R. W. Stott, *The Baptism and Fullness of the Holy Spirit* (Downers Grove: InterVarsity Press, 1964) pp. 30-32.

working day. Salt is not salt only when it is all collected together in the salt cellar. It is equally salt when distributed throughout the meat of society to preserve it from corruption.

The Christian family and the Christian home is a basic unit of the Christian congregation. To those with a scientific education, a useful model of this can be found in the relationship of electrons, atoms and molecules. The complex protein molecule of the congregation is made up of a number of atoms each representing different families. In turn, just as an atom consists of a nucleus with electrons revolving around it, so the Christian family consists of individual Christian electrons moving around the parental nucleus, "in orbit" around the mother's knee, as it were.

Some Limitations of Peer Group Christianity

The Christian individual should take his place, then, first in the basic family unit and then in the larger unit of the congregation. He is not just a little individualistic electron buzzing around at random in a youth organization, an example of what I sometimes call "beta-radiation Christianity!" Some of the very youthful congregations that we meet in places like Singapore or Manila, where the population explosion results in a relatively high proportion of young people in society as a whole and frequently an even higher proportion in the new, emerging congregations, illustrate this deficiency. Many of us have been considerably helped by the youth organizations of various kinds in which we have grown up. But we must also appreciate their limitations compared with a full-orbed, congregational Christianity.

Sometimes the goal of maturity set before teenage Christian peer groups seems inadequate. A mature Christian, it seems, is one who prays and reads his Bible daily, who memorizes verses, gives out tracts and witnesses like mad. This is excellent as far as it goes. But the goal is only that of becoming a mature teenage Christian. This deficient, peer group Christianity needs to be enriched by the corporate emphasis. In other words, let's have higher and fuller long-term goals. We should pray together in our groups about the Christian homes we long to have and the children we long to bring up to serve Christ, and we must also pray about the congregation in which we will play our full part as effective and fully functioning members of the Christian body.

So, while it is wonderful indeed to see a meeting full of young people, I think it is even more wonderful to see a congregation where the families are grouped together row by row—there are three generations of the Wong family, and just behind them are the Tans, and on the other side the Chans, and behind are the Chews! Here surely is a prayer goal for young people in terms of true Christian maturity.

Unfair to the Unmarried?

Some unmarried readers may feel a little hurt by this emphasis upon the family as the anticipated goal of the normal Christian life. As in the world of the New Testament, so in Asia and other parts of the world, it is extremely rare to find unmarried people. Japanese parents who did not arrange suitable marriages for their children would be regarded as thoroughly irresponsible. In the West, however, it is not uncommon to find unmarried adults. Sometimes it is because they feel that the Lord has called them to remain unmarried, and to be "eunuchs for the sake of the kingdom of heaven" as Jesus said (Matt 19:12), and thus to be free to give their whole attention to the things of the Lord (as Paul expressed it; 1 Cor 7:32-35). Others would have preferred to be married but have never had the opportunity. Where, then, do unmarried people fit into this atomic model of the mini-congregation?

1. In Ephesians, Paul is giving illustrations of various relationships within the Christian community—married couples, children and parents, servants and masters. These categories are not exhaustive and are not intended to exclude free men who have no masters, couples who may have no children or men without wives or women without husbands—not just bachelors and spinsters, but also widowers and widows. Paul is merely giving three examples of some typical relationships involved within the community.

2. This is primarily a problem for first-generation Christians, for in later generations unmarried people are still fully in orbit in their own parental atomic family with their brothers and sisters, nephews and nieces, *etc.*

3. The model does not entirely break down. Apparently, what makes silver such a good conductor is the considerable number of free-electrons present. The unmarried similarly play an important part as 'free electrons' within the metal of the church, conducting the power of God to work in the world.

4. Even for unmarried first-generation Christians we are able to say that the congregation as the household of God provides

for them a wonderful extended family in which they may feel wanted and at home and have a satisfying role to play. All of us know any number of outstanding unmarried people who make a tremendous contribution to the growth and up-building of the congregational body through their sacrificial service. Not only are they themselves blessed by being members of the extended family of the household of God, but they also contribute much to the warm reality of the congregational fellowship. In this way everyone knows—young and old, married and single, widow and widower, child and orphan—that they belong wonderfully and delightfully to 'the household of God'. We need to remember that both marriage and being single are temporary states, for in heaven we neither marry nor are given in marriage (Matt 22:30), and that both states are described in 1 Corinthians 7:7b as a "special gift" (the word is *charisma*).

The Family a Divinely Instituted Unit of Community

In many parts of the world today, Christians are becoming increasingly interested in experiments in Christian community. This has been to some degree influenced by sociological interest in the commune and the kibbutzim, and the fear that the nuclear family is too small to provide the stability of the extended family environment that existed before the contemporary pressure for limiting world population by birth control became widespread.[4] Many have felt that some family substitute needs to be found, especially for the many parents bringing up children in the absence of the other partner, lost through death, divorce or desertion; not to mention the need of lonely unmarried persons.

The family has been under fierce attack from humanists of various kinds. Thus, in a book called *The Death of the Family*, David Cooper launches a savage attack on it as a bourgeois institution, arguing that, while children require fathering and mothering, they do not necessarily require mothers and fathers. Christian young people, reacting against thoughtless affluence and the irresponsible accumulation of wealth, have

---

[4] Dennis Bloodworth describes how his wife grew up within a vast walled enclosure in China where 'lived, ate and slept four generations of Liang family with their wives, their concubines, their children, and their numerous servants—about 800 souls in all'. She herself was the "eighth child of the seventeenth son of the patriarch." See *Chinese Looking Glass* (Danvers, Massachusetts: Farrer, Straus & Giroux, 1969), pp. 106-108.

tended to revolt against suburban living with its captive wives chained to household drudgery and baby minding while the husband makes a career. In its place they look for new patterns of a more Christian lifestyle that is more communal.

Suburban values are:

```
Independence
Privacy
Possessions
```

These are regarded as bourgeois and sub-Christian. It is alleged that true Christian values are:

```
Interdependence
Community
Sharing
```

All this sounds great, but experiments tend to founder in frustration and are abandoned. Some time ago I met a young Christian married couple, both still students, who had set up house with another student married couple and several unmarried people. They confessed to a sense of failure, feeling unspiritual because they could not settle to this communal way of living. They had moved in straight after the honeymoon, in spite of advice to make their own home and to establish their own relationship first. They were discovering that they still required some measure of independence, privacy, and a minimum of personal possessions in order to develop their own autonomy and identity as a Christian couple. Had they waited until children had arrived they would have discovered yet further problems arising from the fact that their children would not know to whom they were answerable and whose discipline they were to accept. Idealistically the concept sounds impressive, but in practice it hits problems. Biblically, the need for a man to "leave father and mother" and to "cleave to his wife" is important.[5] The married relationship is given a very exalted status in Scripture, as an expression of the relationship between Christ and the church (Eph 5:22-33). In Corinthians, as we have already noted, marriage is described as a *charisma* or (spiritual) gift (1 Cor 7:7b). At a more practical level, Chinese wisdom represents peace by a combination of ideographs showing one

---

[5] For an excellent explanation of what this "leaving" and "cleaving" means in marriage see Walter Trobisch, *I Married You* (New York: Harper & Row, 1972), chapter 2.

woman under a roof, and though there were very large extended families, usually each wife had a separate establishment.

The example quoted above should encourage us to exercise considerable caution in entering upon experiments. There are apparently widely divergent opinions in Israel at large about kibbutz education. Even on the most basic issues there is little consensus between kibbutz leaders and those most critical of the system.[6]

If there are a very wide divergence of opinions and a lack of assured results among those who have been experimenting radically in communities, then we need to do a good deal of thinking and reading if we are not to repeat the same sad mistakes in other experiments. Both in Soviet Russia and in China there appear to have been real misgivings about the results of a forced communal existence.

'Mixed flatting' is often an issue discussed by students. We are not talking about situations which may be merely an excuse for license. Even non-Christians living in such commune-type flats frequently have strict rules about relationships. It is often a rule that, when two members within the group form an exclusive emotional relationship, one or the other must leave, since such exclusive relationships spoil the whole arrangement. Certainly where Christians enter upon such a mode of living based upon idealized notions of community it seems essential that there should be definite rules and clearly accepted leadership based upon biblical morality and wise Christian common sense. There have been sad instances where in such communities of both sexes, including married couples, people have become attracted to members of the opposite sex other than their own partners, and Christian marriages have been threatened. We must insist strongly that the Christian family is not a bourgeois cultural concept, but a divine institution and the basic unit within the Christian congregation.

This does not mean that established Christian couples (not honeymooners still building their own identity and lifestyle) should not consider keeping open house when possible in order to include others in need. There are families endeavoring to help solo-parents in this way. Others adopt honorary aunts, uncles and grandparents, all of whom are made to feel welcome to call, or to stay for longer or shorter periods, and so to enjoy the extended family situation. It seems essential, however, that communication between the marriage partners and a measure of privacy for the couple and for the children with their own parents, should be

---

[6] Bruno Bettelheim, *The Children of the Dream* (Basingstoke, United Kingdom: Macmillan, 1972), p. 290. This is the most interesting evaluation of the results of a kibbutz upbringing on children and is very helpful for people interested in the development of communities.

regarded as necessary for the healthy development of their own relationships, in order to build a secure environment which they then may be able to share with others. Some measure of separate living accommodation is essential.

In special circumstances, the provision of Christian communes led by married couples who are childless, or whose own children are grown-up, for young people from broken homes or drop-outs from the drug culture may be beneficial. But there seems little biblical justification for young people to leave their own Christian homes, ignoring the clear commands of obedience to their own parents, and voluntarily to subject themselves to those to whom God does not command it. There may be value also for couples whose marriage is under strain to become members temporarily of a Christian community, using it as a substitute extended family for therapeutic reasons. But for the reasons given above it would seem important to maintain a measure of family privacy and autonomy. We must be clear in our own thinking that the congregation is a community established by God who calls us together. We recognize also that the Christian family is a responsibility which we must fulfill and which must take priority. Any other voluntary association such as a community must be secondary to this. If involvement in some kind of commune is hindering the relationships of a married couple or of their children, then the relationships must assert their priority. If families, in order to help, take others into their home and then find they are too much to cope with for a long period, the problem must be discussed with the congregation as a whole, so that others may help to share the burden and give relief.

In stressing that the congregation should be a community, we are not suggesting that it needs to become a monastery or ghetto. The Christian community is a very open community, where homes are open to one another, while each remains a significant mini-congregational unit within the larger body. Experience shows that very tight Christian communities are not always ideal. Theological colleges and large institutions like mission hospitals are almost notorious for the problems that arise when the saints are forcibly communized. However spiritual and committed as Christians they may be, difficulties inevitably arise unless they carefully give their own married and family life proper priority.

Christian community is different from communalism. The local church is not a commune, and the Christian family remains its fundamental unit, although other communal groupings may from time to time be found helpful, especially for individuals deprived of a normal Christian home themselves. For all that is said above, it seems clear that we need both independence and interdependence, privacy and community, possession and sharing.

> Independence plus interdependence
>
> Privacy plus community
>
> Possessions plus sharing

Heavenly Speculations?

The novelist John Wyndham has some interesting fictional speculations about community. The *Midwich Cuckoos* are a group of intelligent children, all conceived the same night, who can communicate with each other to such an extent that information learned by one member of the group is shared by all the others, which speeds up the process of education considerably! It affords an interesting picture of the contribution each member of a Christian community ought to make to the common good. In another book of his, *The Chrysalids*, there are a group of mutants, whose members scattered through society find they are able to communicate with one another by thought transference without using audible words. The members of the group gradually become aware of one another and become a community on a kind of permanent walkie-talkie hook-up! Each remained within their own situation and helped one another as they confronted various problems, including persecution.

The church is more like the second kind of scattered community, linked with one another through their common communication with the throne of grace. The mutual independence and interdependence of these groups, speculative though it is, reflects something of what we ought to experience in the body of Christ.

In heaven, "they neither marry nor are given in marriage;" there is no need for the procreation of children and the physical expression of the love relationships would seem to be superseded. I remember my recently married sister remarking that heaven could not be heaven if there were no marriage there! This reminded me of C. S. Lewis's illustration of the child who, told that grown-ups enjoyed going to bed together, asked whether they eat chocolate there! Just as the child could not imagine any joys transcending eating chocolate, so we may find it hard to appreciate the possibility of joys transcending those of marriage. It does seem possible, however, to conceive of a heavenly relationship between groups of people which may transcend the properly exclusive and God-ordained marital relationship between one woman and one man on earth. Here we see through a glass darkly and then face to face. But however much we may be tempted to speculate, we must insist that, for human life here on earth, the human family is a God-given institution to be respected and enjoyed to the full within the total context of the new developing Christian community. This will find its perfect fulfillment only in heaven with the Lord. We anticipate that heavenly love will transcend all earthly joys and go beyond an exclusive two-person relationship. But this is strictly for heaven! A letter was received by the Far Eastern Broadcasting Association from mainland China in December 1968 in which the correspondent said, "I have said that to lose her would be like losing my hands and feet. This is not an evil feeling. May I ask, don't you people have love between husband and wife? Of course, we should love God more, but it seems to me these two kinds of love must have some relation." What this Chinese Christian expresses is what the Bible says about "every family in heaven and on earth," and the fatherhood of God (Eph 3:14, 15), and husbands and wives reflecting the mutual love between Christ and his church (Eph 5:22-33). There is indeed a connection between these two kinds of love. Christian marriage and the Christian family are the God-ordained units of the congregation, and as Christians we should resist all erosion of Christian values by secular and Marxist humanists.

Conclusion

The Christian family is to be seen as the congregation in miniature. Those who are chosen to rule in the congregation as elders must first prove themselves in ruling their own homes as a mini-congregation. "He must manage his own household well, with all dignity keeping his children submissive, for if someone does not know how to manage his own household, how will he care for God's church?" (1 Tim 3:4, 5). As Christians deeply concerned to develop the new community, let us see that the perfecting of the new community must begin in the home, in our relations with our life partners and with our children. The life of heaven is to be tasted first in the mini-congregation. Bearing in mind the various qualifications suggested above, we should seek within the larger extended family of the congregation to hold out that family joy to others who for various reasons may not have such a Christian family themselves. We must ensure that our churches are not mere institutions which gather for meetings, but are in fact genuine, warm and loving communities which will provide the kind of environment that will enable us to glorify God in beautiful lives lived together.

Our consideration of the Christian home as the basic congregational unit naturally leads us on to think about other kinds of relationship, and particularly those of the Christian at his daily work in secular society. Of this, Christian students provide a particular illustration.

Chapter 7 - The Church and the Student

*Being sent on their way by the church, they
passed through…* (Acts 15:3a)

There is serious danger that Christian students will not only under-value the church during their student days, but that they will also form bad church habits during their student years which may seriously impair their lifelong usefulness to the church of Jesus Christ. They find the fellowship of their peer-group so much more satisfactory than that of the local congregation. Moreover, they are used to organizing their own Christian Union program so that they feel thoroughly involved in and fully responsible for it. By contrast, even the more go-ahead evangelical churches may sometimes seem rather traditional and institutionalized, and the students who attend have little or no say in what goes on. They thus tend to become critical spectators rather than eager participators.

In the limited time available during a college course, student energies tend to be concentrated, quite rightly, upon taking the unique opportuni-ties for evangelism and fellowship within the university context. In addi-tion, some loyalty to chaplaincies or to college chapels may be expected of them. As a result, some students become casual about church atten-dance, some attending different congregations, morning and evening, some going only once on a Sunday and some apparently not attending any church at all. I hasten to add that the casual, haphazard approach is not encouraged by more thoughtful Christian students but is the prod-uct of undisciplined Christian thinking and the individualistic approach already described as characteristic of much Western Christianity, exagger-ated often by secular impatience with the "establishment."

This raises a whole number of important issues. What is the relation-ship between the church universal and the church local? What is the relationship of independent Christian societies of all kinds (including college and university Christian Unions) to the local church? There have been instances where such groups have treated themselves as, or even declared themselves to have become, a local church. What, then, are the proper marks of a local church and when does the group which is not a church become a church? These are all issues which need to be thought out very clearly if students are to get the best possible value out of their Christian Union activity and their relationships with local congregations during their college years.

The Goal of Student Groups

The real test of student group effectiveness is whether or not the group is preparing the members properly for the role which they will need to play in a local congregation for the next fifty years. It is dangerously easy for Christian Unions to think of themselves as an end in themselves, concerned only about evangelism in the university or college context. This, while certainly an important and essential ingredient of CU activity, is surely only a part of it. We must always be asking ourselves: "How effectively are we preparing our members and those who profess conversion for spending their lives in the service of our Master, and particularly in fulfillling his will with regard to building his church?"

It cannot be too strongly stated that student organizations are never an end in themselves but are for the *church*. They add to the church's numbers by effective evangelism on the campus. They train their members for Christian service, initially within the university or college context, it is true; but not in preparation for a whole lifetime of service in the churches. The student life span of three or four years is a very brief and fleeting part of a total life lived for Christ. The long-term effectiveness of a Christian Union is to be measured, not in terms of numbers attending meetings, nor even of the numbers of those converted, but by the number of its former members who, as a result of its teaching and training, become useful and fruitful members of local congregations when they graduate or qualify.

The goals of a Christian Union are often extremely clear to its founding members. Subsequently, as they leave, their place is taken by others who begin attending meetings of the now existing Christian Union. The original, strong, responsible sense of "we" and "us" can be replaced in the course of three years by a tendency to refer to the CU as "it" or "them." The original founders felt thoroughly responsible, integrated and involved. Now it has degenerated into an amorphous body of individual Christians who go along to meetings of "it" and who often feel critical of "them," namely the committee which has been appointed from among some of the more enthusiastic to organize the meetings of "it." Once this degeneration has taken place, it becomes easier for members to regard the Christian Union as existing for its own sake, instead of recognizing that it is only a small part of God's total building of the church universal.

Is Any Group of Christians "the Church?"

In the most general sense that, wherever two or three are gathered together in the name of Christ, he is present with them, we may regard such a gathering as a part of the church. As we suggested earlier, even a slender crescent moon may be described as 'the moon' even though only a small part of it is visible.

This does *not* mean, however, that wherever there are groups of Christians, they necessarily exist together as a local church. It is thoroughly reprehensible for people to evade their biblical responsibility to be involved and integrated members of a local congregation by claiming piously, "I am a member of the universal church and that is all that really matters!"

I would like to defend this dogmatism from New Testament usage. For example, the passage already quoted about Christ's presence with the two or three (Matt 18:20) is most significant. In the context, the Lord Jesus tells us that, if our brother sins against us, we should go to him privately and seek reconciliation (v.15). If he will not listen we take one or two others with us so that "every charge may be established by the evidence of two or three witnesses" (v.16). If he refuses to listen, then Christ says, "tell it to the church. And if he refuses to listen even to the church, let him be to you as a Gentile and a tax collector" (v.17). The two or the three are not regarded as "the church;" that is identified as a larger body, which is nevertheless locally circumscribed in such a way that it can be "told" something and the erring individual can "listen" to it. This particular passage obviously makes a clear distinction between the small group and "the (local) church."

The usage in Acts is also decisive. Scripture does not support the idea that any small group of Christians who happen to be thrown together can be regarded as "a church." After the dissension and debate with the

Judaizers, "Paul and Barnabas and some of the others" (Acts 15:2b) were appointed to go up to Jerusalem to the apostles and the elders about this question. Then we are told (Acts 15:3a, 4a) that "being sent on their way *by the church*, they passed through…When they came to Jerusalem, they were welcomed by *the church*…" Both the group that sent them and the group that received them are described as churches, but the travelling group of "Paul and Barnabas and some of the others" are not so described. On a later occasion, Paul was travelling from Philippi to Troas together with a substantial party consisting of Sopater, Aristarchus, Secundus, Gaius, Timothy, Tychicus and Trophimus (Acts 20:4) together with Luke, certainly (notice the "we" of v.6) and probably Titus (also included in the "we"; *cf.* 2 Cor 8:23). Here were an outstanding group of Christian men, as far as gifts and qualifications are concerned, who might well on the basis of a casual (but unbiblical) definition be regarded as "the church on the boat." But a very clear distinction is maintained between the travelling party, which is never described as a church, and the churches which they visit. Subsequently the same party arrived at Miletus, and Paul sends to Ephesus for "the elders of the *church*," but in what follows "the church" is clearly regarded as being back in Ephesus and not at the conference of the elders with Paul and the party of those with him.

There does seem to be a biblical distinction, then, between what may properly be described as "a church" and various other *ad hoc* groups of Christians, even though all of them, as true believers, are part of the church universal.

What Then is a Church?

Let me suggest a number of marks which it seems to me must normally be present before a 'group' truly becomes a 'local church'.

1. *Location* The expression "local" church reminds us that an *ad hoc* or traveling group does not seem to be described as a 'church' in the New Testament. When the word is used it is usually associated with a particular town or city, or even a house, so that definite location seems to be basic.

2. *Organization* Titus was left in Crete "that you might put what remained into order, and appoint elders in every town as I directed

you" (Titus 1:5), so that a certain minimal organization seems to be necessary to the local church. Anthony Norris Groves wrote:

"For myself I would join no church permanently that had not some constituted rule. I have seen enough of that plan, of everyone doing what is right in his own eyes, and then calling it the Spirit's order, to feel assured it is a delusion."[1]

3. *Authority* It seems that a congregation ought to have elders, as in the verse quoted above from Paul's ministry in Galatia. A number in the region of Pisidian Antioch had been converted (Acts 13:48) and are described as "the disciples" (13:52). The converts at Lystra are also described as "the disciples" (14:20) and in Derbe they also "made many disciples" (14:21). Significantly the word "church" is not used of any of these new groups of Christians in Galatia until we read, "and when they had appointed elders for them in every *church...*" (14:23).

The qualifications for an elder include ruling his own household well, a good reputation in society as a whole, an aptitude for teaching (see 1 Tim 3:2 and Titus 1:5-9). A local church, then, would appear to require elders (in the plural) who will be mature men of some standing in the local community.

4. *Discipline* The elders of the church at Ephesus are told to "be alert" (Acts 20:31a) and to "Pay careful attention to yourselves and to all the flock, in which the Holy Spirit has made you overseers, to care for the church of God" (Acts 20:28). They were to be sentinels and shepherds who would guard the flock the flock from its enemies and care for their well-being. Christians are exhorted to obey their leaders and to submit to them, "for they are keeping watch over your souls, as those who will have to give an account. Let them do this with joy and not with groaning" (Heb 13:17b). Paul inquired of the Corinthians, "Is it not those inside the church whom you are to judge?" (1 Cor 5:12b). As well as positive teaching to build up the faith of Christians, there is also the corrective ministry of admonition to bring individuals to repentance and to deal with the spots and blemishes in the body of the church. We also find the stronger word "discipline" implying a more physical restraint and encouragement to godliness.

---

[1] Harriet Groves, *Memoir of the late A. N. Groves* (London: Nisbet & Co., 1856), p. 420.

5. *Initiation* Baptism will normally be administered in a local congregation, though it may be administered in other special circumstances (see Acts 8:36-38; 16:33).

6. *Communion* This is the new covenant meal where we are reminded of God's covenant promise: "I will be your God, and you shall be my people." The breaking of bread (Acts 2:46) is one of the regular meetings "when you assemble as a church" (1 Cor 11:18ff.), although probably not necessarily restricted to congregational occasions.

7. *Teaching* There are various words for teaching used frequently in the New Testament, and elders are required to be "apt to teach". In his address to the Ephesian elders, Paul emphasizes that he "did not shrink from declaring to you anything that was profitable", or from "declaring to you the whole counsel of God" (Acts 20:20, 27). It is probable that from where Paul was speaking to the elders the sound of the creaking of canvas and ropes would carry from the Miletus harbor. Paul is using a nautical word, meaning that "he did not trim his sails." In his teaching he carried a full spread of doctrinal canvas. Fellowship alone without authoritative teaching is not enough.

8. *Spiritual gifts* It is significant that the exercise of spiritual gifts is spoken of in a strongly congregational setting. A peer group of comparative novices could well be deficient in exercising all the gifts which, according to the Bible, would seem to be shared across the whole spectrum of age and experience in the congregation.

9. *Families* It has already been pointed out in the previous chapter how basic families are to the structure of the congregation (Eph 5:21, 22). It is a qualification of an elder that, if he has children, they be believing (Titus 1:6). A group of students or any other youthful peer group cannot properly be a local church in a fully biblical sense until the group includes married couples with children.

10. *Universal in membership* There is no such thing in the Bible as churches for rich men and churches for poor men, churches for intellectuals and churches for dunces. Local circumstances, as when different languages are spoken, may mean that the membership of a church cannot be fully representative of all races, classes and conditions of men. But as far as it is possible, a church must aim to be all-inclusive (see 1 Cor 1:11-13; Gal 3:27-29).

Is There Any Scriptural Warrant for Groups Which are Not Churches?

Whereas some Christians have tended to magnify the role of societies to an extent which has been detrimental to their members' playing a full and proper part in the local congregation, others have gone to the opposite extreme of being such good 'churchmen' that they question the right of any Christian group to exist outside the local church. At one time a certain missionary began to teach that Christians in assemblies in the country where he was working should withdraw from school and university Christian Unions, the Scripture Union, Youth for Christ and so on. What scriptural justification could be found for such activities which, while they might claim to be within the scope of the church universal, lie outside the control and direction of the local churches? It has to be freely admitted at once that the direct biblical justification for such groups and activities is not great, although I personally believe, as you will see, that it can be allowed from Scripture.

Throughout the whole of church history much new work has been begun, by the grace of God and under the guidance of the Holy Spirit, through initiatives taken in the first instance by individuals. These initiatives, having been greatly used and blessed by God, subsequently found favor and approval on the part of the church.

The first example of such independent initiative in Scripture and in church history is when

> some of them, men of Cyprus and Cyrene, who on coming to Antioch spoke to the Hellenists also, preaching the Lord Jesus. And the hand of the Lord was with them, and a great number who believed turned to the Lord (Acts 11:20, 21).

Up to this point, the scattered Christians were "speaking the word to no one except Jews" (Acts 11:19b). The Jerusalem church, indeed, had been critical of Peter's going to Cornelius even though he had the strongest guidance. Later they insisted that Gentile converts be circumcised and observe the Jewish law. Had the matter been left to the church officially, therefore, it seems very unlikely that there would have been any unanimity, or even a majority, in favor of taking the gospel to the Gentiles. But these individuals took a definite initiative which resulted in an extension of the gospel and a bringing in of Gentiles to the kingdom of Christ. The Jerusalem church reacted by sending Barnabas, and one gains the impression that he was sent to check up and to make sure that these new developments were desirable. The new Antioch congregation had grown, and in their turn had sent out Paul and Barnabas. This resulted in the establishment of new congregations in Galatia before the Jerusalem church made any clear statement indicating approval of the Gentile outreach.

The same kind of independent action has been repeated throughout church history. Even such respected groups as the Church Missionary Society or the Church's Ministry among the Jews were originally not official Anglican projects at all but were initiated by godly individuals such as Charles Simeon working with others of like mind. Only subsequently did they receive tacit official approval. The same is true of many other interdenominational missions and societies specializing in particular forms of outreach which have only later and gradually become accepted and appreciated by denominational leadership. In these men of Cyprus and Cyrene, there would seem to be a charter and a genuine biblical warrant for such independent initiative outside the local church.

The second biblical strand which seems significant is the recognition that there may be groups of two or three which are not meetings of the local congregation as such. Exhortations to Christians not to forsake the assembling of themselves together and to exhort one another *daily* suggests that small *ad hoc* Christian group activity was as much a feature of the first century as of the twentieth, even if not on the same scale.[2]

Factory and office Christian Unions as well as those in schools, colleges and universities would seem to fall into this pattern of the small group which, while blessed with Christ's presence, and a true church meeting, is not technically a meeting of the (local) church as such. At the same time, to concentrate on such extra-congregational activity to the almost total neglect of the local church, as has been sadly characteristic of certain young people's organizations in recent years, surely lies right outside a truly biblical Christianity. The elder of a Kuala Lumpur assembly commented sadly that the three student organizations competing with each other in the university had a very weak doctrine of the church. One of these groups was even holding Sunday meetings at the same time as the local church gatherings, thus drawing their student members away from full and proper participation in congregational activity.

While fully recognizing the conflict of loyalties and the difficulty of apportioning limited time between such a variety of Christian activities, it is not really a choice between the good and the bad, but more frequently

---

[2] See Stibbs, *God's Church*, p. 98.

the problem of deciding between the good, the better and the best. The Christian student needs real wisdom in knowing how to respond to the considerable variety of Christian activities in which he is invited to participate.

The Student and the Local Church

While appreciating tremendously the fellowship, opportunities for evangelism and teaching that we have in our college Christian Unions, we need to recognize that, as a peer group activity, it does not provide us with the wisdom and balance that comes from a full spectrum of age and experience. Christian Unions are great 'swingers' from one extreme to another. The student generation is short—on average three or four years long. Trends which take a decade or two to develop at the congregational level are accelerated furiously in the student context. A student group which last year was solemnly Calvinistic has this year somehow become rabidly Arminian!

Throughout our lives we all need the help of experienced elders, wise pastors and teachers. We need discipline, counsel and advice. We may get excellent advice from Christian friends of our own age group, but if we value the full exercise of spiritual gifts across the whole spectrum of the congregation, we shall recognize that problems which loom large for us, because we are meeting them for the very first time, may well be understood by an experienced minister who has helped countless scores of others to come through similar problems.

The important thing is that we should determine not to be satisfied with anything less than real involvement. Merely attending churches in the town where we are studying, loosely attached as a spectator of services and an auditor of sermons, is totally unsatisfactory. Certainly such churches maybe crowded on Sundays with an enthusiastic group of Christian students. The danger, however, is that they may regard this as merely another Christian Union meeting in a different hall with the opportunity to listen to a good message and to be spiritually fed and encouraged, while remaining utterly detached from local congregational life. This is a very bad habit to get into!

In certain circumstances, from a long-term point of view, it may be better for the student to ally himself with a smaller congregation, possibly less popular amongst students, but one where he or she may become fully involved in the local congregation and play a real part in its life. Careful balance needs to be found here. There are always those who would seek escape from the more difficult task of witness to their fellow students in favor of being the big man from the college throwing his weight around among the local Sunday School kids (like the big monkey with the little monkeys).[3] A Christian student must be fully involved as a witness in his college situation, in co-operation with his fellow Christians, but he must also seek to play some part in local congregational life.

After the first few weeks of term, having seen what local churches there are, the student should make a serious approach to the minister and elders of a congregation requesting that during his time at college or university he might be received as a member and be fully involved within that congregation. There would be a number of possibilities.

1. Some students will already have strong ties and membership in a home church. These should be retained, but that does not mean that they cannot be accepted as associate or student members of the congregation they attend during term. In Britain an interesting body known as MUT (Ministers in University Towns) gives its attention to discussing this problem of relationship between the student and the local church in the university town and some such congregations make definite provision for the student in this way. Would that more did!

2. When it is clear that a student will spend far more time with this congregation than he can possibly spend with that in his home town, he should definitely consider transferring his membership, so that he can be known to belong to the congregation and can have some say in its affairs. For many medical students and nurses this may be the wisest course.

3. There remains the case of those who are converted while at college and may previously have had no church connection. Those responsible for instructing them should see that, from the very beginning, they are aware of their responsibility to be fully integrated into a local congregation. Not being members of a church in their home town, it would seem they ought to become fully integrated into the life of a local church in the area where they are studying. This naturally means entering through the proper channels of Christian initiation appropriate to the denomination of their choice.

---

[3] See chapter 6: "The Church as a Family Community," under the heading "Spiritual Isolationism."

Students and Elders

Student rebellion against authority and against the older generation generally may encourage similar thinking among young Christians, so that they become impatient of both instruction and elders. But the Bible teaches that we need elders. As individuals we do not do just as we like, or what we 'feel led' to do, without consultation with the rest of the church, both old and young, married and unmarried. It is not unknown for new Christian groups and so-called 'house churches' to be formed, not for spiritual reasons, but simply because the people concerned are inspired by a secular spirit of rebellion against all authority. Admittedly there may be rare occasions where young people are genuinely forced to leave a congregation, not for doctrinal reasons, but because older people do not like some of their cultural *mores*, such as long hair and unconventional clothing. But such comparatively trivial matters should not be allowed to become a reason for division. No-one, whether young or old should leave a church until they have tried their hardest to remain in it, and people should never go out unless they are forced out and can do no other.

There is a danger that young people who see through the conventional cover-ups of lower standards by more senior people in the congregation will feel so frustrated that they rebel and speak angrily. They may even react much as teenagers do in their own homes sometimes, and deliberately try to shock the older generation. The problem here is that the elders, responsible for church discipline and for doing everything decently and in order, will feel threatened in their leadership, or feel that the unity of the body is imperiled, and will over-react in a heavy-handed repressive way in order to curtail the revolutionary ideas of the young people.

Just as Scripture tells children to obey their parents, and also warns fathers not to "provoke your children to anger" (Eph 6:4a), so young people must make a conscious effort to remember the biblical commands to give respect to the properly appointed leadership; and the leadership, in its turn, should take care not to antagonize its young people. They must listen to and try to understand each other. When we are older we become realistic to the point of cynicism. But when we are younger we see so clearly the faults and the humbug of the older generation. Both groups must accept that the other group is also part of the body. We may regard them as "less honorable" (1 Cor 12:23a), but we must not treat them as though they are not parts of the body and therefore of no account. The young must not despise their elders or write them off. Correspondingly the elders must not despise and patronize the young or treat them as less than people, merely because they are still young. They are also Christians, and just as much members of the body. Why say all this? Because it is tragically common to find congregations which have lost their young people because they antagonize them. Genuine Christians have been cut adrift because of a failure to see them as being also part of the body. The scriptural injunctions are clear:

> Obey your leaders and submit to them, for they are keep-
> ing watch over your souls, as those who will have to give an
> account. Let them do this with joy and not with groaning, for
> that would be of no advantage to you (Heb 13:17).

We have to give account of ourselves, but our leaders have to give account of how they have exercised their responsibilities towards us. Even Timothy, though an apostolic delegate appointed to a position of authority, was told not to rebuke an elder but to appeal to him as a father (1 Tim 5:1a), and was also told not to accept an accusation against an elder unless there were two or three witnesses (1 Tim 5:19).

> Likewise, you who are younger, be subject to the elders.
> Clothe yourselves, all of you, with humility toward one
> another, for "God opposes the proud but gives grace to the
> humble" (1 Pet 5:5).

Young people may also need to be reminded that their "elders" are not just older people who have been a blessing to them! We cannot appoint our own elders from father figures whom we happen to like! Elders are appointed in the local church to which we belong, and we have to accept that congregation as it is, not as we might prefer it to be. We may not appreciate all the particular fads or viewpoints of those who are elders, but the fact remains that they are proper elders and Scripture commands that we should respect them as such.

After Leaving—What?

The graduate or college leaver who as a student found his fellowship and activity solely within the Christian Union must beware of spending the rest of his life in a state of adolescent nostalgia because he no longer finds the same degree of fellowship or enjoys the same quality of teaching as that which he formerly experienced with his fellow students. Because during the formative period of his life he learned somehow to survive without vital integration into a local congregation, he finds a curious vacuum in his life; he no longer has the Christian Union to prop him up, and yet has little experience of being integrated properly into a local church. He may have become accustomed to an unusually high standard of preaching and speaking, both in the Christian Union and in the privileged city churches he has attended which frequently draw particularly able and eloquent ministers. Unless he corrects his attitude he may remain permanently dissatisfied and critical of the less well-known, but equally faithful, ministers of the gospel in an ordinary local congregation. Should such a person remain congregationally maladjusted, the increase of pressures due to growing responsibility in business life, not to mention the early, busy years of marriage with a home and small children, provide ample excuse for decreasing attendance at the local church, and even sometimes defection from it. The reason for such backsliding is that he has not learned as a student the importance and significance of corporate growth in the new Christian community.

The proper attitude for the person who has said goodbye to student life is entirely different: he can rejoice in simplification of his Christian commitments. Now at last he is living in one place, not in two, so that he is in a position to throw himself whole-heartedly into the life of the local congregation. He is old enough now for full adult participation and for accepting practical responsibility within the church.

Isn't our future church involvement something that students should pray about before they qualify or graduate? Our praying about the future is often restricted to our life work and our life partner. Once these are settled it becomes a matter of looking for a nice house and a nice school for the children. In all the busy-ness of moving, surely the most important thing to be praying about ahead of time is to be sufficiently close to a good local church where the young family can be blessed, and where they can play a full part in blessing others. Frequently, however, church involvement is an afterthought. The finding of a pleasant house and acceptable schooling arrangements comes first. The couple discovers, too late, that the nearest evangelical church they would like to attend is several miles away, so that it takes real effort to get to mid-week or other special meetings, and it is quite inconvenient for small children to get to Sunday School or teenagers to get to their own peer group activities at the church.

Even when we ourselves deeply desire to be fully involved and to make a real contribution, it is not always easy. In some numerically large churches, or in flourishing and famous evangelical congregations with an outstanding pulpit ministry, it may still be difficult for the new arrival to discover any significant role which he may play. We must not allow this to discourage us. Just as personal growth and sanctification are not easy, congregational growth and sanctification are also anything but easy. If we want to see the new community perfected we shall have to "work out our own salvation with fear and trembling" (Phil 2:12b). We may feel inadequate to realize our ideal for the congregation. We may meet considerable resistance from people with a conventional view of "church-going." We may be misunderstood by congregational leaders who do not share the same vision. Writing to the Galatians, Paul agonizes, "I am again in the anguish of childbirth until Christ is formed in you!" (Gal 4:19). There is a struggle and an agony to be experienced in bringing the new community to life.

Yet surely here is something worth laboring for. What a difference there is between the Christian who potters drearily along, "going to church" with no particular aim in view, and the one who, in the midst of a busy life earning his bread, butter, and jam, and bringing up a family, devotes his life and energies to the building up of the new community, striving with all his heart and soul for a beautiful church, "without spot or wrinkle or any such thing" (Eph 5:27b).

Reasons for Choosing a Congregation

We have endeavored to suggest that dissatisfaction with the church, so far from being deplorable, is something to be expected in the healthy Christian. If we are not aware of the imperfections of the churches as they now are, then there is something badly wrong with us! The Old Testament prophets were "angry young men" exercising under the inspiration of the Holy Spirit a corrective ministry among the people of God. The apostle Paul was manifestly deeply disturbed and dissatisfied with the state of the churches: that is why he wrote his Letters. John's letters to the seven churches (Rev 2-3) display the same sense of deep dissatisfaction with the churches as they are. Clearly, then, we must be realistic and not expect a perfected church now, but see that this is God's intended goal. We recognize that the building is under construction and that the bride is being prepared, though as yet she is anything but ready for the Bridegroom's return!

What then, are the factors we should take into account when deciding what congregation we should join, assuming that we have some choice in the matter? Are there any guidelines to help us or questions which we should ask ourselves? May I suggest the following:

1. If I am a young Christian I need a solid foundation of biblical teaching in order that I may rethink my attitude to everything. To sit under a ministry which is not Bible-centered is therefore foolish in the extreme. It is not enough that Bible verses be quoted occasionally as a kind of hook on which to hang the scattered thoughts of the preacher. I need to ask myself whether the Bible is really being taught and expounded in this congregation.

2. Even if I am an older Christian I need to ask whether this congregation is a place to which I could happily bring fellow students, or professional colleagues or business clients. Can I be sure that, when I bring non-Christians with me, they will really hear an explanation of the gospel proclaimed in a way which they will understand and to which they may respond?

3. Young married couples in particular must ask, "Is this congregation a place where my children will be properly taught and given a solid foundation of biblical teaching?" In the hope of seeing revival and change and transformation, I may, as a mature Christian individual, be able to tolerate a great deal of divergence from the historic Christian faith,[4] but my responsibility to my own children is such that, not only do I not wish them to hear anything harmful, but I want them to receive something which will be positively helpful and encouraging.

Nevertheless, as we have indicated, we must expect a church made up of redeemed sinners to have problems—spots and wrinkles and the rest. In any case, in some more rural situations there may be little choice.

What, then, should I do in this kind of situation?

1. We should be very cautious before we write "Ichabod" ("The glory has departed") over any congregation (see 1 Sam 4:21a).

Yet as to our liberty in Christ to worship with any congregation under heaven where he manifests himself to bless and to save, can there be in any Christian mind a doubt? If my Lord should say to me, in any congregation of the almost unnumbered sections of the church, "What doest thou here?" I would reply, "Seeing thou wert here to save and sanctify, I felt it safe to be with thee." If he again said, as perhaps he may among most of us, "Didst thou not see abominations here, and admix-ture of that which was unscriptural, and in some points error, at least in your judgement?", my answer would be, "Yea, Lord, but I dared not

---

[4] A young Christian couple with strong faith might be able to give five years working in a not particularly evangelical congregation before children are of an age to be adversely affected.

call that place unholy where thou wert present to bless, nor by refusing communion in worship reject those as unholy whom thou hadst by thy saving power evidently sanctified and set apart for thine own." Our reason for rejecting the congregations of apostate bodies, is that Christ does not manifest himself among them in their public character, though he may save some individuals as brands plucked from the burning. To these churches we cry, standing on the outside, "Come out of her, my people; come out of her."[5]

2. We should not leave a congregation without having prayed, if possible with other like-minded people, for revival and transformation though God's working both in minister and in people. I have met remarkable instances both in Wales and in the United States where ministers entered into an experience of the new birth and their whole ministry was transformed as a result of the prayers of a believing remnant in the congregation. It is not enough to be critical and to leave in distress if we have not done our utmost through prayer to see the situation transformed.

3. We ought not to leave until we have done our utmost to give a gracious and winsome testimony for a truly biblical faith and experience. There may well be in the Young People's Fellowship, for example, a group of others as dissatisfied as we are ourselves and longing for fellowship and encouragement. We must not be merely negative, therefore, but seek positively to have an influence for good, praying for progress rather than regress in the congregation.

4. I do feel that, if it is the Lord's guidance that we should leave, then we should not sneak out quietly in cowardly fashion without explaining to the responsible leaders of the congregation why we are doing so. In love and sorrow, as well as in fear and trembling, we ought to go to the minister and church leaders one by one and explain to them why we are regretfully leaving. It may be that the Lord will use this to make them realize how other people react to their current ministry and leadership. Obviously the manner in which we do this will be crucial. If we merely go with a view to having a flaming row and bitter words, then we are not likely to achieve much.

---

[5] A. N. Groves, *On the Principles of Union and Communion in the Church of Christ*, quoted in F. Roy Coad, *A History of the Brethren Movement* (Grand Rapids, MI: Eerdmans, 1968), p. 116.

We also need to realize what a solemn step this is. Anthony Norris Groves, that man of truly Christian spirit who was one of the early leaders of the Open Brethren, wrote on this same subject:

> To the question, are we not countenancing error by this plan?, our answer is that, if we must appear countenance error, or discountenance brotherly love, and the visible union of the church of God, we prefer the former, hoping that our lives and our tongues may be allowed by the Lord so intelligibly to speak that at last our righteousness shall be allowed to appear… so long as Christ dwells in an individual, or walks in the midst of a congregation, blessing the ministration to the conversion and edification of souls, we dare not denounce and formally withdraw from either, for fear of the awful sin of schism, of sin against Christ and his mystical body.[6]

5. There is the problem that, if the local church is the church universal in local circumspection, then there ought not to be different denominational tabernacles competing within one small local community. This may well be true, but which of the possibilities would be the most viable option would vary from place to place.

Pause for prayer

This seems a good point at which to take stock of our present church involvement. We need to repent of our failures, our casual attitudes, our cynical pessimism, and particularly because "we have left undone those things which we ought to have done."

Let us dedicate ourselves afresh in the fullest possible commitment and participation in the life of the local congregation and let us ask the Lord to hold us firmly to that goal, whatever the discouragements.

---

[6] Quoted in F. Roy Coad, *op. cit.*, p.116.

Chapter 8—The Church and its Services

We "worship by the Spirit of God and glory in Christ Jesus and put no confidence in the flesh" (Phil 3:3).

In our stress upon church as a new community, a "love demo" on the march, we must not run to the opposite extreme of undervaluing the actual gathering together of the *ekklēsia*. Now that we are aware that "church" is far more than "attending services," this does not allow us to become superior critics, despising weekly gatherings as a form of institutional observance or mere cultic, ritual performances. We must not react to our new view of the church in a wrong way.

> It is well to remember that neither St Paul nor any of the apostles ever "went to church." They never saw and probably never imagined a building built and set apart exclusively for Christian worship.[1]

While this is absolutely true, our fresh view of the *ekklēsia* as a community of heavenly citizens does not mean, therefore, that we undervalue opportunities for gathering together. On the contrary, we now value our gathering together as a congregation much, much more because we understand its purpose in a new community perspective. Because the church is a community, worshipping seven days a week in the totality of its work and lifestyle, the times of gathering together become much more precious and not less. This is well expressed by Emil Brunner:

> It would be incorrect to say of the *ecclēsia* that it becomes real only in the act of assembly…the first Christians were conscious of their membership of the *ecclēsia* even when the latter was not assembled for the cult. They understood their life to

[1] Mark Gibbs and T. R. Morton, *God's Frozen People* (Louisville, KY: The Westminster Press, 1964), p. 27.

be a continuous act of worship apart from the cult altogether, when each individual in his particular walk in life, in the everyday world, in the family circle or in his daily avocation, offered his life to Christ his Master as a sacrifice, well-pleasing to God.

Brunner goes on to qualify this by showing that services and meetings have a vital part to play in helping Christians to realize their community, and that such meetings are essential if the community is to grow and develop.

> These meetings of worship had precisely the dominating purpose of building up the body of Christ. The assemblies were edifying, not in our colorless sense of the word, but in the strict and literal sense of building up... For only here occurred the actual realization of the body's communion in Christ which is the presupposition for the reality and witness of each individual's membership in the isolation of his worldly calling.[2]

It is such gathering together that enables the community to recognize itself as the body of Christ and that nourishes the life of the whole community.

An individual body is a body all the time, not just at mealtimes. But meals are essential if that body is to continue in health, to grow and to develop to maturity.

A family is a family all the time, not just when it meets together for meals. It is when the family is doing things together that its ties as a family are strengthened. You look at the faces of your parents and your children with fresh love and joy, and a fresh understanding of what it means to belong to each other.

A congregation is a congregation all the time, even when it is scattered among secular society, but it is when it assembles together as the Lord's people on the Lord's day that it is able to realize and appreciate its unique community—and most significantly when it meets to eat together symbolically in the Lord's Supper.

---

[2] Brunner, *The Misunderstanding of the Church*, pp. 60f.

The Supreme Value of Meeting with Others

If meeting with a single fellow Christian brings joy, how much more meeting with the whole community. Dietrich Bonhoeffer was later destined to spend time in prison isolated from Christian fellowship, and it is therefore all the more interesting to read him writing on the subject of *Living Together* in 1938:[3]

> The prisoner, the sick person, the Christian in exile, sees in the companionship of a fellow Christian a physical sign of the gracious person of the Triune God. Visitor and visited in loneliness recognize in each other the Christ who is present in the body: they receive and meet each other as one meets the Lord, in reverence, humility and joy…If there is so much blessing and joy even in a single encounter of brother with brother, how inexhaustible are the riches opened up to those who by God's will are privileged to live in the daily fellowship of life with other Christians…It is true, of course, that what is an unspeakable gift of God for the lonely individual is easily disregarded and trodden under foot by those who have the gift every day. It is easily forgotten that the fellowship of Christian brethren is a gift of grace, a gift of the kingdom of God that any day may be taken from us…It is grace, nothing but grace, that we are allowed to live in community with Christian brethren…

All of us appreciate fellowship and sharing with one other individual. Properly that individual benefit ought to be multiplied many times whenever we meet together with a whole congregation of other Christians. We have already discussed the problems of individualistic Christians being "congregationally maladjusted." The writer to the discouraged Hebrew Christians, tempted in the midst of trials and chastening to give up their faith, reminds them to "consider how to stir up one another to love and good works, not neglecting to meet together, as is the habit of some, but encouraging one another, and all the more as you see the Day drawing near" (Heb 10:24-25). In difficult days they needed more than ever this dimension of meeting Christ in the fellowship of other believers. We are in no sense belittling the preciousness of individual fellowship with the Lord when we remember that he himself taught a special revelation of his presence, "where two or three are gathered in my name" (Matt 18:20a). The same is also true in the larger congregation. "For we are the temple of the living God; as God said, 'I will make my dwelling among them and

---

[3] The English translation was published under this title in 1954 by Harper and Row.

walk among them, and I will be their God, and they shall be my people'
(2 Cor 6:16b).

It is not, of course, the mere act of assembling together which brings
blessing. It is the fact that, when Christians gather together as a congregation, God himself draws near in a special way. Just as under the old covenant the glory of the Lord filled the Tent in the wilderness and the Temple
in Jerusalem, so now the glory of the Lord is revealed in a particular way
in the new temple made up of living stones. We have already suggested
that the great prayer of Paul in Ephesians 3:16-19 is to be understood
predominantly in a congregational sense. Here is another verse which we
have commonly expounded in an individualistic way but which is deeply
enriched when we apply it to the local church "family."

> And we all [how could we ever have missed the congre-
> gational understanding of this verse!], with unveiled face,
> beholding the glory of the Lord, are being transformed into
> the same image from one degree of glory to another. For this
> comes from the Lord who is the Spirit (2 Cor 3:18).

It is when we meet with others in the congregation that we meet with
the Lord who himself has summoned us together. It is his *ekklēsia*.

The Character of Christian Meetings

It is not just the reason for our meeting together but the manner in
which we meet together which is significant. And this is a significance
which, sadly, many of our meetings have lost.

> It is unfortunately true to say that church worship and rule
> have devolved to a disproportionate and unbiblical extent
> upon the ministrations of one man, i.e. the minister or pastor.
> Worship has been taken over by "services;" praying by the
> whole church has been superseded by prayers on their behalf
> by the preacher; the exercise of spiritual gifts to a large extent
> has become the province and prerogative of one elder, i.e. the
> preaching elder. In other words, the exercise of the collective
> gifts in the church has largely fallen into disuse, and there is
> no doubt that one of the main contributors to this state of
> affairs has been the rise of the "one-man ministry." There is
> no question but that the Lord has provided adequate gifts for
> his church, and that even today these gifts are discernable in

many. Unfortunately, however, in the present order of things, many of these gifts have no opportunity to be exercised…[4]

Brunner makes the exceedingly valid point that the character of the meeting is essential to the building up of the body.

> But it was not only the act of meeting in itself which was so significant for the realization of the individual membership of the body of Christ; it was rather the character of the meeting which served this very real purpose of incorporation. These meetings were not merely… a coming together and a being with each other, but they aimed at making out of the mere assembly an act of vital cooperation (1 Cor 14). They signify the performance of something in fellowship, a reciprocal giving and taking.[5]

This, of course, is precisely what the one-man band type of congregation is not. One, member of the body is active, but all the rest are passive. The heart certainly has a crucial function in circulating blood to other members, and gifted pastor-teachers have a biblical function to perform in perfecting all the saints for the work of service (Eph 4:11f). But there is surely an essential point here that the very nature of such a gathering expresses the mutual interdependence of the actively participating members with each other in a functioning body.

Again let me quote from Emil Brunner's book. This is how he describes the way in which the New Testament church functioned:

> Co-operative action in fellowship might be regarded as its decisive feature. It is especially emphasized that *all* were active in it. What we have already discovered concerning the intrinsic structure of the community—namely that it knows no distinction between the active and the passive, between those who administer and those who are recipients—this is evinced anew in the character of divine worship. Each made his contribution and for this very reason no one was allowed to monopolize the hearing of the assembly. Thus everyone could have his turn (1 Corinthians 14:31). This cult, therefore, knows nothing of the distinction between priests and laymen; its members are aware that they form a priesthood

---

[4] Emil Brunner, *The Ministry and Life of the Christian Church* (Wales, United Kingdom: Evangelical Movement of Wales, 1968), p. 28.

[5] *Ibid.*, p.61.

(1 Peter 2:9) and this holy priesthood is built up of each and all (1 Peter 2:5).[6]

It is surely useless to protest that to allow such spontaneity is to make an end of "decency and order." The New Testament insists on decency and order but does not see these as the enemy of spontaneity. If the community is to be realized in the character of Christian meeting, and if, indeed, this is a truly biblical concept, then we cannot merely give mental assent and lip service and yet continue to perpetuate our fossilized forms of service.

This idea of the congregation expressing its "body-life" is biblical: "Is not the bread which we break a sharing in the body of Christ? Since there is one bread, we who are many are one body; for we all partake of the one bread" (1 Cor 10:16-17, NASB). C. K. Barrett argues convincingly that "sharing in the body of Christ" here is not a reference to the physical body of Christ, but rather a reference to the church as Christ's body just as in 1 Corinthians 12:27.[7]

Because the individuals present have all been united to Christ by faith, they are one body, and this is evidenced by the one loaf in which all partake.

Those who have determined to take 1 Corinthians seriously in their worship, as the Christian Brethren have always done, and as the best in the charismatic movement are now doing, would all agree with Brunner. There is no necessity to tie corporate involvement in worship either to the Lord's Supper only, or to spectacular gifts and speaking in tongues. Merely allowing the congregation to make responses to versicles, to sing psalms and hymns and to ask two to read the lessons does not really seem to meet the New Testament requirement. Still less does the typical non-conformist hymn sandwich where the congregation's vocal involvement is limited further to singing hymns and saying a brief "Amen" to the minister's praying. The whole context of "body-life" teaching has profound implications for worship, and the body exercises itself and enjoys its diversity most obviously when it is engaged together in this spiritual activity.

We have already drawn a parallel between the individual body sustained by occasional meals and family life strengthened by its family gatherings. A military analogy underlines the same point. If the church militant is to be effective when dispersed and battling in a hundred separate engagements in the field, then instruction and training on the parade ground is

---

[6] *Ibid.*, pp61f.

[7] Barrett, *Corinthians*, p. 233.

an essential prerequisite. Its effectiveness in battle depends on the development of *ésprit de corps*, an awareness of itself and a pride in its ability to co-operate together with precision and order when assembled on its own barrack square. The Brigade of Guards is famous for its prowess on the field, but would relate this to its disciplined perfectionism developed by countless hours of drilling on parade. An army is not just for parade ground drilling and instruction, but it is this which conditions a group to become an effective fighting force. The congregation does not exist merely to be instructed and to sing hymns to one another. But our gathering together is of crucial importance for our effectiveness when we go out to live for the glory of God and to stand firm in courageous witness for him in the battlefield of the hostile world.

The Poverty of Protestant Worship

When a new Christian group or meeting is started there is at first an attractive freshness and spontaneity. But how rapidly this falls into a fixed form! Our minds run so easily in ruts. Soon the raising of hands aloft, One Way signs, J-E-S-U-S yells, hand-clapping and pious murmuring become the keen clichés of the new orthodoxy. There is a deeply rooted problem here, for, whatever our denominational or non-denominational tradition, our meetings so easily become stereotyped. Soon we scarcely need to think and concentrate; our minds are free to roam and often do.

I shall never forget talking with a Filipino Bible school lecturer who said sadly, "What do we Protestants know about worship? When I go past a Roman Catholic church and hear them singing, all the Spanish and Filipino blood in me responds. What do we Protestants have? We have a song leader, who stands up front, raises his arms and says, 'Let's all *sing*!'"

He went on to blame this poverty on the pattern imported by Protestant missionaries. Many congregations use the hymn sandwich format. Some even print the order of service in such a way that the hymn numbers can be added (just to harden the ruts a bit more!), and regard the service as 'the preliminaries' to the sermon. This has become the commonest cultural from characterizing English-speaking countries. How refreshing it has been recently to become a member of a congregation where the reading and exposition of Scripture come first, and then worship arises out of our response to hearing the Word of God. Amusingly the sermon-at-the-end pattern accepted by so many nonconformist churches derives almost directly from the Anglican pattern to which they are not conforming!

I am not for a moment suggesting that formless worship is to be preferred to formal worship, though one has little patience with liturgical antiquarians. It is the attitude of heart of the worshippers which is the fundamental thing.

True Worship

C. S. Lewis, in a characteristically refreshing passage, shares his early doubts about how it could be that God himself demands that we should praise him. He felt that it was like saying, "What I most want is to be told that I am good and great."

> I had never noticed that all enjoyment spontaneously over-
> flows into praise unless (sometimes even if) shyness or the
> fear of boring others is deliberately brought in to check it.
> The world rings with praise—lovers praising their mistresses,
> readers their favourite poet, walkers praising the country-
> side, players praising their favourite game—praise of weather,
> wines, dishes, actors, motors, horses, colleges, countries, his-
> torical personages, children, flowers, mountains, rare stamps,
> rare beetles, even sometimes politicians or scholars. I had
> not noticed how the humblest, and at the same time most
> balanced and capacious, minds, praised most... I had not
> noticed either that just as men spontaneously praise what-
> ever they value, so they spontaneously urge us to join them
> in praising it: "Isn't she lovely? Wasn't it glorious? Don't you
> think that magnificent?" The Psalmists in telling everyone
> to praise God are doing what all men do when they speak of
> what they care about.[8]

The language "fabulous," "fantastic," "smashing," is the language of spontaneous praise in recognition of worth-ship. That's worship! Praise and worship are the mutual sharing and enjoyment of all that has blessed us. Just as when sitting with friends one shares the best of books that one has read, records that one has heard, birds that one has seen, butterflies one has caught, and fish that got away, so Christians when they meet together want spontaneously to talk about the astonishing riches of God's character and grace, and his attention to the intricate details of salvation to a degree beyond our ability to ask or think.

---

[8] C. S. Lewis, *Reflections on the Psalms* (San Diego, CA: Harcourt, 1961), p. 80.

William Temple defined it beautifully as follows:

> Worship is the submission of all our nature to God. It is the
> quickening of conscience by his holiness; the nourishment
> of mind with his truth; the purifying of imagination by his
> beauty; the opening of the heart to his love; the surrender of
> will to his purpose—and all of this gathered up in adoration,
> the most selfless emotion of which our nature is capable and
> therefore the chief remedy for that self-centeredness which is
> our original sin and the source of all actual sin.[9]

It's when we worship the Lord together on our knees with our brethren,
rejoicing in all his winsomeness and wisdom, and when Temple's definition is transmuted into the corporate dimension—*our* consciences, *our*
imaginations, *our* hearts, *our* wills—that we begin to see the Lord corporately, sanctifying the congregation as we worship him, progressively
transfiguring our values so that they begin to approximate to his. Thus,
we get our perspective straight and our values sorted out.

Fellowship Together Before the Lord

Israelites who lived at a distance from Jerusalem were commanded
to turn their tithes into money before they journeyed to the Temple to
worship and then, upon arrival, to "spend the money for whatever you
desire—oxen or sheep or wine or strong drink, whatever your appetite
craves. And you shall eat there before the Lord your God and rejoice,
you and your household" (Deut 14:26). That is a startling use for one's
tithe! The intention is plain, however. Even under the law there was to
be rejoicing in being together in the presence of the Lord. Perhaps the
Chinese with their love of feasting can also point us to the goodness of
meeting together and enjoying one another's company. I remember once
being privileged to attend the weekly Sunday feast of a Chinese Christian
family which, after morning worship and the breaking of bread, met
together for lunch—all three generations of them, including the children.
In Japan, the Koganei church always remained together for a congregational lunch—just sticky buns and instant noodles. But what a delightful
time of fellowship and sharing together.

Many congregations lack such fellowship. Murmuring polite nothings
to each other, even if associated with the traditional non-communicat-
ing handshakes before and after the service does not really provide the

---

[9] William Temple, *Readings in St. John's Gospel* (London: St. Martin's Press, 1939), p.68.

fellowship and knowledge of each other which a congregation requires if its body-life is to develop. I shall never forget being with an Anglican congregation using the form of service known as Series Three, when suddenly I saw the minister approaching me as the visiting preacher, and every member of the congregation turned to his neighbor, shaking him by the hand warmly and saying, "The peace of the Lord be with you." Up to that point the service seemed to have meandered along. But now suddenly everything came alive. We had recognized one another as people together in the presence of the Lord, and how enriched we all were as we then went on to meet together around his table.

Unfortunately, in many congregations this just doesn't happen. People are content week after week and year after year to "attend services." They become acquainted with other members of the congregation sufficiently to recognize their faces but without, in many cases, ever knowing them as people. When Paul had his stop-over in Troas, with the message that lasted till midnight, the interruption following the fall of Eutychus, the breaking of bread, the eating of a meal together and further conversation until dawn, we gain the impression of a depth of fellowship and enthusiasm which our congregations today need just as much as they did. Hendrik Kraemer writes:

> Along what ways is it possible to express in new forms of fellowship and community, the fact (which is now rarely evident) that the church is a Christocentric fraternity?…How do we break through the sociological imprisonment which is so often spoken about…? The indirect approach by really *being* communities of mutual upbuilding, of witness and service, by building in the desert of modern life genuine Christian cells, is the one indicated.[10]

Wherever one goes today there seems to be the same longing in the hearts of God's people for the church to realize itself as a new community through reality in its worship. Christians need to become aware that they are not solitary searchers after truth, isolated wrestlers with temptation, and lonely worshippers confined within the limits of their own subjective, religious experience. They must recognize themselves as members of 'the body', the new community which is now being perfected, and which will arrive at final salvation together as God's triumphant people.

---

[10] Hendrik Kraemer, *A Theology of the Laity* (Louisville, KY: The Westminster Press, 1959), pp. 177, 179.

Small-Group Activity

Many congregations today are beginning to see the importance of meeting in small groups, particularly for Bible study. Some excellent booklets have been written on the subject.[11] We have already noted that the meeting together of two or three is specifically mentioned by the Lord Jesus himself. We must not assume, however, that the method will be automatically successful. Those who have been members of small Christian Unions will be familiar with some of the snags—the leader who insists on delivering a long monologue, the theological expert who frightens everyone else into silence by his show of learning. But where such problems arise the answer is to correct the method, not to abandon the approach.

It seems vital, however, that we should try to relate such small groups to the biblical importance of the family which we have already emphasized. An interesting book called *The New Face of the Church*,[12] by Larry Richards, suggests that one of the weaknesses of the otherwise excellent American all-age Sunday school has been that it has isolated people into their peer groups so that parents and their teenage children are instructed separately and apart from one another, thus weakening rather than strengthening the Christian family structure within the congregation. He thus recommends that house groups be made up of, say, five households including not only the parents but also their adolescent children. The value of such group Bible study, where each member can make fresh discoveries for himself or herself, and where the Holy Spirit has illuminated their minds as they have grappled with the meaning of the text rather than having its message handed out in pre-digested form by the religious professional, seems from an educational point of view to be a better method of learning. Each member is helped by the fresh discoveries of the others, and the wise leader will know when to press for practical application and when to steer the group back from unprofitable side issues and irrelevancies. I am not one of those people who believe that everything should be buttoned up in a method carefully and systematically set out on paper. I believe that where groups meet together and are determined to make them work, they will learn by their mistakes and functioning together as members of the body, and will keep on reforming and improving their group activity. When the group finds its meeting dull and boring, or its members

---

[11] I would recommend especially *Breakthrough*, by Tom Rees (new edition, Hildenborough Publications, 1972), and two books by David Adeney, *Action Groups* (Christian Witness Press, Hong Kong) and a sequel, *Small Groups in Action* (The Way Press, Singapore).

[12] Published by Zondervan in 1970.

becoming apathetic, then it can repent together in prayer and seek the Lord's help in perfecting what it is seeking to do.

Pause for Action

At this point a little self-examination may be a good thing. Is our congregation already making provision for such group activity? If not, is there something practical which we could do to spark off a real development of such 'body-life' in our church?

Are we really giving our gatherings of the congregation all we have got? It is so easy to degenerate into a critical spectator! Do we need to repent and determine afresh that, whatever the weaknesses are, we are going to worship the Lord with all our heart, and to be not merely passive but active in sharing with others all the wonder of what the Lord is, and has done and is doing for us, his people?

Chapter 9 - The Church and Missions

The church exists by mission as fire exists by burning. - Emil Brunner

The implications of what we have been saying about the beautiful people of God and the necessity for our fullest involvement with the local congregation in its body-life must also be worked out in relation to our thinking about mission and missionary societies. It ought to be inevitable that concern for the "church in local circumscription" should lead to a worldwide concern for the universal church. The Christian minister who might have claimed, "The parish is my world" now begins to say with John Wesley, "The world is my parish!" Newbigin comments that,

> In the thinking of the vast majority of Christians, the word 'church' and 'mission' connote two different kinds of society. The one is conceived to be a society devoted to worship and the spiritual care and nurture of its members. It is typically represented by a large and ancient building. The other is conceived to be a society devoted to the propagation of the gospel, passing on its converts to the safe keeping of 'the church'.[1]

The relationship between the two societies is far from clear. Newbigin goes on to say:

> It is taken for granted that the missionary obligation is one that has to be met *after* the needs of the home have been fully met; that existing gains have to be thoroughly consolidated before we go further afield; that the world-wide church has to be built up with the same sort of prudent calculation of resources and costs as is expected of any business enterprise. Must we not contrast this with the kind of strategy that the

---

[1] Newbigin, *The Household of God*, pp. 143f.

New Testament reveals, which seems to be a sort of determination to stake out God's claim to the whole world at once, without expecting that one area should be fully worked out before the next is claimed?

It is my conviction that a new discovery of the body-life of the new community will utterly transfigure the relationship between church and mission.

The Goal of Missionary Work

We live in days when even some people who ought to know better think of missionary work as primarily a matter of providing teachers for theological colleges and technical experts for medical and social services overseas. Students commonly inquire how they may use their professional qualifications and skills in overseas situations. It is difficult to avoid the impression that the whole purpose of missionary work has been entirely lost sight of! If what we have been discovering in earlier chapters is correct, then the great goal of all missions is building the church. It may occasionally be true that providing agricultural and technical experts may be of assistance to Christian work in some countries. But surely the aim of the whole operation must be the planting and perfecting of new colonies of heaven, new congregations of beautiful people.

Parallel with this mistaken conception, that missions now exist only to provide technical expertise, there is the apparently contradictory idea that the best way to do missionary work is to go out for two or three months in a summer, or possibly for as long as a year (!), in order to distribute Christian literature, to witness, and if possible, to lead some people to faith in Christ. Both these misconceptions arise from a failure to recognize that the goal of missions is the building of the church.

Now obviously for a student to spend his summer vacation in this way is quite useful. It may also be helpful if people make themselves available for one or two years for similar work, particularly in countries where the language spoken is one of the former colonial languages like English or French. But in countries which have retained their own language, even an intelligent individual is unlikely to master that language in less than eighteen months at the very least and this raises real questions about the effectiveness of the work that can be done on a short-term basis. The point I am trying to make, however, is that such work, while excellent in its own way, is incomplete and inadequate in its understanding of its proper goals.

"An unchurchly mission is as much a monstrosity as an unmissionary church,"[2] writes Leslie Newbigin. If in our own homeland our chief goal is to build the church because that is God's great purpose in the world, then it follows that that purpose is equally as important in any other country. The work of literature distribution, including the widespread dissemination of the Bible, and the leading of individuals to a personal experience of faith in Christ, is a necessary preliminary to the gathering together of new congregations of God's people. But we have not really completed our work unless these individuals are then able to realize their involvement in the body of Christ by being gathered together into a local congregation.

In western countries, in order to compensate for the deficiencies of the institutionalized churches, many excellent interdenominational and much-used youth organizations have come into existence. Their work is to complement that of the churches. Often their particular aim is to reach young people whom the church is failing to reach. In order to avoid any appearance of competition with the churches they have become entirely extra-congregational, and thus sometimes give the impression of being indifferent to that whole crucial area of Christian doctrine which we are studying. In order to avoid being controversial, they have often said nothing about the importance of the church at all.

When such attitudes are carried to what have been traditionally called "the mission fields" the result is activity which is so much outside the churches as to be quite irresponsible. Missionary work has to be church-centered if it is to be effective.

The Para-Ekklesia Syndrome

Well-meaning individuals are constantly arriving in overseas countries with a strong sense of call to engage in some form of specialist missionary work. For some, the all-important thing is to increase the output of Christian radio programs. For others the main task is the widespread distribution of Christian literature. Others again feel that the most significant kind of missionary work is that among the strategic intellectuals from whom will come the future political leaders and formers of public opinion, so they feel called to specialize in work with university students. Others see, quite rightly, that Bible teaching is vital and therefore they

---

[2] *Ibid.*, p. 148.

concentrate on setting up Bible colleges where people may be taught and instructed in order to minister to others.

Now all this can be extremely useful, and there is a great deal to be said for a diversification of Christian effort along these various lines, and the use of every possible means to bring people under the sound of the gospel, provided that such groups do not lose sight of the end in view, namely the planting and perfecting of churches! But unless such work is to be continued by foreigners indefinitely, the question soon arises, who is to make the Christian broadcasts and write the Christian tracts for use in that particular language and culture? Usually there are well-qualified national Christians who can be employed to do such work. But how is that radio work to be more effectively followed up? By local churches, whose members are prepared to visit contacts and integrate them into Christian congregations when they profess conversion. Who is going to distribute all our Christian literature? Clearly the most desirable thing is that it should be done by national Christians, who are able at the same time to witness intelligibly to their own faith, in their national language, and who are thus able to follow up such distribution effectively. Similarly, if a self-supporting literature program is to be developed, it must depend very heavily upon producing literature for Christians who will pay for what they read. It is virtually impossible to build up a self-financing program, paying its own way, by producing evangelistic material for non-Christians. The development of an effective evangelistic literature program depends inevitably upon Christian congregations and church members who are prepared to make use of the literature as it is produced.

In student work also, one rapidly learns that where there are good, strong local churches with good biblical teaching, there you have an excellent source of keen and well-instructed Christian student leaders who will be effective in witnessing and working within the campus situation. But where there are no such churches, and the work has to depend upon individuals who have been converted almost *in vacuo* as it were, one becomes acutely conscious of how such believers struggle and flounder because they do not have the help and encouragement of good local Christian congregations. Their very survival as Christians at all is a miracle of the working of God's Holy Spirit in that situation. Successful student work is inevitably parasitic upon the churches in the early stages. Later, of course, we expect that it will become reciprocal and that those who have been trained in the university or college situation will throw their weight into their local churches, while some of the best may go into Christian full-time ministry and bless the churches in that way.

Anyone trying to start a new Bible school rapidly becomes aware that they are entirely dependent upon existing congregations to send promising Christians to train in their school, and that they are usually in varying degrees dependent also upon those same congregations to provide the finance to support those students. Similarly, when the students have been taught and trained, problems immediately arise if there are no congregations who wish to engage their services, the more so if trained individuals expect from the outset to become "full-time" religious professional workers.

In other words, it is not just that the church *ought* to be central to missionary work, but that it inevitably *is* central to missionary work and the real effectiveness of all such ancillary work depends upon the degree to which that work is church-centered and church-pivoted, not merely in formal statements of principle, but in its everyday thinking and practice. For the purpose of public relations and fundraising in wealthier countries, the work is often described, I am afraid, as though it were entirely isolated from everything else. The contrary is in fact true. Where it is isolated it is ineffective; but where it is integrated it can be exceedingly fruitful to the building up of the body.

The Missionaries' Cultural Spectacles

The reason for this book is the fact that some Christians have no real understanding of the church at all. One major problem in missionary work is that we missionaries ourselves also have inadequate concepts of the church and export them with us overseas! Inevitably our own expectations, and the goal for the church which we have in view, will be shaped and colored in terms of our own experience within our own culture in the congregations of our acquaintance.

Some missionaries have an *institutional* concept of the church. They anticipate setting up an organization which will conduct services at regular intervals, modelled along the lines of the traditional hymn sandwich pattern with which they have been familiar. We cannot help this: what we have always experienced as "our church" is inevitably going to determine for us what we think "the church" ought to be like. We may be critical in some areas of what we have experienced and seek to improve upon it; but inevitably our own thinking and expectation will be limited by our experience. If we come from North America, we are bound to be influenced by our experience of high quality real estate and the efficiently organized congregational structure with not just one full-time pastor, but with other full-time workers for Christian education, church music, young people's work and the rest. If, on the other hand, we come from Germany, steeped in Reformation history, we shall think in terms of ancient Gothic buildings, great tolling bells and slow ponderous hymns. I happened to make this comment once at a conference in Thailand and was greeted by loud laughter from a section of the congregation which I quickly observed to be made up of German missionaries. I subsequently discovered that the reason for their embarrassed mirth was that they had recently imported three large bells from Germany into Thailand! Somehow, for them, a church was not really a church unless it had a bell! If this is true in more superficial matters, how much more is it true in our general thinking and expectation about the church we hope to build.

Other missionaries may have an *ivory tower* view of the church. We may have grown up in a small, struggling congregation of saints who have thought of themselves as utterly distinct from, and indeed rejected by, the world all around. The church to us is a kind of ghetto into which we escape from the wicked world outside. When such a view is exported overseas where the new Christians are initially a tiny minority, such a view of the church tends to increase their isolationism.

There is also the possibility arising from all that we have been saying that many missionaries inevitably will have an *individualistic* view of the church. There is this terrible danger that we will perpetuate the distorted view of the form of Western Christendom in which we ourselves have grown up.

Here then is our big problem as missionaries. We have to be born somewhere. We are inevitably the product of a certain local, national and denominational situation. We cannot avoid this. But we need freely to recognize this difficulty not only in relation to the doctrine of the church, but to every other doctrine; and to be exceedingly careful that we go back to Scripture, and not to experience alone, in our understanding and thinking about such matters. We shall recognize our limitations and always be ready to accept the possibility that many of our ideas may be culturally rather than biblically determined.

The National Christians' Ear-Filters

If the missionaries' cultural spectacles were the only problem and we could be certain that the national Christian is always right, then it would be comparatively simple to solve all our problems regarding the church by sending all the missionaries home! But we cannot overlook the fact that the national Christian also has his own cultural presuppositions and that he is just as much determined and shaped by his own environment as the missionary has been. One might say that he is wearing a kind of cultural ear-filter. Certain things which the missionary says are totally incomprehensible and rejected in their entirety. Others are received more or less as the missionary intended they should be (although, as we have seen, they may include distorted misunderstandings of the church) while, most dangerously, other things will be thought to have been understood, but will for various reasons have been completely misunderstood.

We must use our imagination. Here are a group of eager seekers being taught in the missionaries' house who have never met even one Christian before, let alone a Christian congregation. They have no concept at all in their mind of what a Christian congregation is supposed to be like. They will build up this picture from what the missionary says, to the extent to which they understand him, and also by what they begin to experience as the new congregation begins to emerge.

Misunderstandings will arise in various ways.

1. *Through mistranslation*

    If there are difficulties in translating *ekklēsia* into English or German, there will be at least equal problems in translating that word into any other language. We have already mentioned the use of the two Chinese characters meaning "teaching association," used not only by the Chinese, but by the Japanese and the Koreans. Inevitably the word used will color the concept which people have in mind when they use it. In this instance it suggests an intellectual circle being instructed by a religious professional. This approximates closely to what many in the West visualize when they think of the church. It ties in wonderfully, from a cultural viewpoint, with the Confucian concept of the teacher and his disciples. It is nonetheless exceedingly misleading and fails to convey the true biblical content of the word *ekklēsia*.

2. *By comparison with known religions*

    We all conceive the new and the unknown in terms of that which is already known and understood. It is almost inevitable, therefore, that Christianity will be compared with known religions, the church building regarded as homologous with the mosque or the temple, and the Christian minister with the imam or the priest. Many such religions involve difficult and archaic language which is used by the religious professional, while the 'laymen' remain passive and non-comprehending spectators. Religion is not necessarily related to daily living but will involve occasional attendance at religious ceremonial. If this view of religion forms an amalgam with a weekly-service-orientated form of institutionalized Christianity, the misunderstanding is further compounded.

The extreme subjectivism of a religion like Buddhism, where the individual's own experience is the only reality, tends to encourage an equally individualistic and subjective form of Christianity.[3] People commonly think by analogy and comparison with known experience, and again this may lead people astray from a true biblical understanding of the church. Subsequent experience in second- and third-generation Christians may enable them to rethink their doctrine of the church and correct it. But if the church has become institutionalized and distorted in the way in which it already has in Western countries, then experience may serve only to reinforce the distortion and misunderstandings.

From what has been said about the problem of the missionaries' cultural spectacles and the nationals' cultural ear-filters, it can be seen that it is not necessarily any easier in new missionary situations to avoid reproducing these misunderstandings of the church which have already taken place in Western Christendom, and still harder to eradicate them once they have arisen.

The Kind of Missionaries Needed

It cannot be too strongly emphasized, therefore, that the kind of missionaries most required in the world today are not the various ancillary workers with specialist qualifications so much as those whose gifts enable them to preach and teach, and to plant and perfect congregations. The so-called "specialists" rapidly become redundant, as they can be very properly replaced by newly trained national Christians. Indeed, it is almost a matter of national pride, as well as of Christian expediency, to ensure that such "prestige posts" are taken over by national Christians as soon as

---

[3] This is not necessarily true of all monistic religious systems, and, I am told, Hindus have a great sense of solidarity with the group, which makes it at least possible for them to understand the concept of Christians being united in the body of Christ.

possible. It is in this context that one needs to understand "Missionary go home!" statements like the following:

> The missionary structure had performed magnificently the role of a successful midwife in helping to bring out into the light of day a new child, which is none other than the rise of the Christian community in the lands of the Third World. But now that the child is born there is no longer any need for the midwife…Now the child is grown up…The day of his independence and maturity has arrived. Therefore, all guardians and trustees must now withdraw…For the missionary movement to do this final act of self-abnegation would be the most fitting conclusion to a long and glorious career of self-oblation…This one final act of self-sacrifice on the part of modern missions is nothing less than the charter of freedom and life for the younger churches. In other words, the best missionary service a missionary under the present system can do today in Asia is to go home![4]

Clearly relationships here are all wrong. The missionaries are thought of as trustees or guardians, or in some measure better qualified and more mature than their fellow national Christians. If either the missionaries or the national Christians think in those terms it is perfectly natural for them to want to end that kind of relationship.

Does our doctrine of the church give us any guidance in responding to this kind of appreciated frank comment? The Letter to the Ephesians speaks not only of national pastor-teachers equipping the saints for the work of service, but also, apparently, of a continuing role for international itinerant apostles, prophets and evangelists. It is possible, of course, to argue that the apostles and New Testament prophets were no longer necessary once the canon of the New Testament was completed. On the other hand, the apostles may be thought of in the secondary and derived sense of the "apostles of the churches" (2 Cor 8:23b, RSV margin) and the prophets in terms of those whose work it is to edify the church (1 Cor 14:1ff., 24, 29ff., 39; see also Acts 15:32). It seems difficult to disregard so great a weight of New Testament teaching about prophecy by relegating it all to a past dispensation! According to Ephesians 4:11-13 this work of apostles, prophets, evangelists together with the pastor-teachers for the equipping of the saints for the work of service to the building up of the body of Christ continues "*until* we all attain to the unity of the faith and

---

[4] Emerito Nacpil, speaking at the Kuala Lumpur Conference of the East Asia Council of Churches.

of the knowledge of the Son of God, to mature manhood, to the measure of the stature of the fullness of Christ" (Eph 4:13).

The establishment of a national church as an evangelistic bridgehead within a country is not sufficient. Some national churches have been established for hundreds of years and are making little or no impact upon the indifferent and unconverted masses of the population. In Japan, for example, though a fine national church exists, there are still more than a hundred million unconverted Japanese. In spite of all we hear of revival in Indonesia, the statistical fact remains that 98% of the Javanese (who make up 50% of the total population of Indonesia) are still without Christ. Peter Wagner has recently shown how missionary enthusiasm for evangelism has become increasingly restricted, because in the World Council of Churches the churchmen have ousted the missionaries, so that church politics receives far more attention than the evangelism of the two billion people in the world who are still without Christ.

> Closely related to this is a missionary slogan which can do more damage than one might think: "My job is to work myself out of a job." The fallacy involved is to project the need for a national to *take the missionary's* place rather than for the national, in his own style, to *lead the national church*. In other words, the missionary tends to say subconsciously, "When my national brethren are well-polished Christians, when they have grown to Christian maturity, when they have graduated from seminary as I have, when they can exegete the Greek and refute the humanists, and when they have a driver's license, I will be glad to turn the work over. I will have worked myself out of a job." If the apostle Paul had been captured by this mentality, I am afraid he would still be in Iconium.[5]

Wagner is chiefly concerned because, as he puts it: "As each new wave of missionaries goes to the field, more are sent *church-to-church*, rather than *church-to-world*." He feels that missionaries have become so obsessed with the church and its structures that they have forgotten to carry on with evangelism. Personally, I feel this is a false dichotomy. The work of the evangelist must certainly continue so that there are always fresh additions being made to existing local churches and, indeed, a constant addition of fresh congregations in areas which formerly were unreached with the gospel. The problem arises because the necessity of congregational

---

[5] Peter Wagner, *The Babylonian Captivity of the Christian Mission* (Self-Published Booklet, Pasadena, 1972), p. 16.

sanctification remains unrecognized. Both the missionary society and the national church have felt that the job is done when some church structure (however small) has been established and church services are being held. If that is all, then certainly the job is done and the missionary must either go home or look for new areas in which to evangelize and plant fresh churches. Our study of the doctrine of the church, however, would indicate that there are still two tasks to be achieved by the international church. One is to reach the unreached with the gospel through evangelistic outreach and the other is to help perfect the saints for the work of ministry in order to build up the body of Christ.

Experience also shows that there is one kind of missionary who is always indispensable and sure of an enthusiastic welcome back. No-one wishes him to go home. He is the individual who is thoroughly church-centered or rather church-pivoted in all his thinking and activity. He may not be particularly highly qualified in any sophisticated specialist category. He is, however, a man with an infectious personal faith who is always leading others to Christ and bringing them into the church. He is always encouraging congregations to start new daughter congregations. He is the kind of charismatic catalyst whose infectious love for the Lord enables the church which has invited his assistance to grow and develop into that kind of perfected new community which Scripture leads us to expect. Anybody anywhere in the world would be foolish to send that kind of Christian worker packing.

We sometimes forget that, while national churches exist in other parts of the world, they may be minute, struggling minorities making little impact upon society as a whole. I am constantly amazed when back home in Britain to discover small villages with three or four functioning congregations. Over vast areas of Japan there may be one tiny congregation serving as many as a hundred thousand people. In Thailand there is only one Christian in a thousand. In Cambodia there is only one Christian in two or three thousand. On the same scale this would mean a congregation of five in a parish of five thousand, or a Christian Union of five in a university of ten thousand. How lonely you would feel! What is remarkable is that, even in those countries where there are strong national churches, there are still open doors and open hearts for missionaries of the right kind such as I have tried to describe. Even in Korea and Indonesia where, numerically, at any rate, the churches are exceedingly strong, there are still invitations and requests for missionaries of any race from any part of the world who could make a contribution of this kind.

Old-Fashioned Side Show?

Our new thinking about the church, however, ought not only to revolutionize our thinking about missionary work abroad; it must also inevitably influence our thinking about the local church and its relationship to that work.[6] As a missionary visiting local churches in various sending countries, I am quite frequently thoroughly depressed by the attitudes I find, even though I recognize them as thoroughly consistent with the misunderstanding of the church we have already described. Wherever you have a vital understanding of what the local church really ought to be, as the new community of beautiful people, there is also a quickened and revitalized missionary concern. But where the church has become institutionalized, then the view of missionary societies has become equally institutionalized, and they are thought of primarily in terms of tedious collections and meeting burdensome financial obligations. The personal element is lost and people find themselves supporting sets of initials. It is scarcely surprising if there is little enthusiasm for praying for missionary bureaucrats and expensive administrative superstructures.

What, then, are the implications of our renewed biblical way of thinking about the church for missionary activity? It follows, surely, that the whole congregation will desire "body-life" involvement with its missionaries. Those members of the congregation who are called by God to serve overseas will not be regarded as dismembered hands or amputated toes who have been whisked off to distant parts, but as a genuine outreach of that local congregation overseas. Some congregations are sluggish creatures like the eight-armed octopus writhing about on the ocean bottom. Others, however, are more like the active ten-armed squid which moves rapidly through the surface waters of the great oceans. It has eight short arms and two long tentacles. These longer arms are able to reach out and secure food at a distance and then bring them back to the shorter arms to complete the job. Similarly, the active church will have its missionary outreach at a distance as well as its own local evangelistic outreach. Those members who have gone overseas will be regarded as extensions of the work of the local congregation. The congregation will not think of it as "their" missionary work so much as "our" missionary work.

---

[6] For a more detailed treatment of this subject see my booklet, *Get Involved in Missions! Some suggestions for ministers and congregations disenchanted with the traditional muddle* (London: Overseas Missionary Fellowship, 1972).

As I have suggested elsewhere,[7] this sense of congregational responsibility for missionary work should be evident from the very beginning. In ordinary secular life, diplomatic representatives are carefully chosen on the basis of their qualifications to represent their country. Even in the world of sport we do not rely on any old Tom, Dick or Harry to volunteer to represent their country in the Olympic Games, but we select the very best athletes available. It is an honor to be chosen and the initiative is taken by others. A study of the relevant New Testament passages showing how Barnabas first went to Antioch and how Saul was first invited to join him, and then show subsequently Paul and Barnabas were sent out from Antioch for the first missionary journey, as well as the later appointments of both Silas and Timothy, all show that the initiative was taken in the first place not so much by the individual as by others in calling them and selecting them for missionary service. The Holy Spirit, who is the author of Scripture, emphasizes the objective calling and involvement of "the body," rather than the subjective call and personal willingness of individuals. How much better it is that a congregation should feel missionary concern together, and seek to fulfill it by looking out from among their own number a suitable Barnabas or Timothy, and asking them to consider prayerfully the possibility of their going overseas in response to the call of their local church. When this is done and the whole of the local congregation has been involved from the beginning, there need be no frantic struggle to maintain missionary interest by appeals for money or prayer. The congregation, who are themselves responsible for those chosen individuals being overseas, will automatically want to ensure that their own missionaries do not starve and that they are adequately prayed for. Because it has become "our missionary work" people will realize that they may participate directly through prayer with those whom they have sent out. It is part of their body-life.

Instead of those rather depressing missionary exhibitions with their collections of anthropological bric-a-brac and dog-eared promotional literature, much of which is taken away because it is free and most of which is thrown away without ever having been read; instead of the constant struggle to maintain missionary activity as a peripheral program for the super-saintly few, missionary work becomes the principal passion of the whole congregation. Instead of an impersonal foreign missions program with a host of missionary societies clamoring competitively (and at times, incidentally, spending a great deal of Christian money on employing public relations firms to ensure "success"), there is an inevitable deep

---

[7] See Michael C. Griffiths, *Give Up Your Small Ambitions* (Chicago: Moody Press, 1972), pp.17ff.

concern and desire for involvement with the members of the congregation who are fulfilling the congregation's obligation overseas. Certainly the existing channels of experienced missionary societies will continue to be used; but those societies will not need to spend their energies and finance in trying to whip up the flagging enthusiasm of local churches for their work. The local church will be so involved already because of its concern with its own members that the missionary society need no longer be self-consciously concerned with "public relations" at all. That becomes necessary only when the church has become cold and institutionalized.

Missionary Prayer Groups

We have already spoken of the importance of small-group activity within the local church. Congregations may choose to organize themselves in a variety of ways, but certainly even quite small congregations have found it possible to organize continent-wide prayer groups for Africa, Asia, Latin America, *etc.*, so that the local congregation's concern for the progress of the gospel everywhere is demonstrated by its prayer for the whole world. Alternatively, it may be preferable to synchronize missionary prayer groups with the existing house groups rather than add a separate layer of organization. Their prayers will inevitably tend to be focused upon the particular work being undertaken by the missionaries sent out by that congregation and upon other missionaries serving overseas known to them personally. The various societies will continue to provide information and requests for prayer which will be immensely useful to such groups. But the meetings will be more congregation-centered than society-centered, eliminating competition between missions, and giving a much more balanced view of total Christian endeavor in any country than the present system, under which one is frequently given the mistaken impression that the missionaries of a particular society are the only people there! I remember being once asked in Canada if I knew "the missionaries in Japan." I then discovered to my mingled amusement and distress that these worthy people had imagined that the four couples sent out by their particular denomination were the *only* missionaries serving in Japan. I was happy to point out that there were, in fact, more than two thousand others, mostly of similar evangelical conviction, engaged in the same work. Their sense of involvement was excellent, but the nonsense of their ignorance was not!

There is always this danger that our view of the church overseas will be distorted because of our limited knowledge. Ensuring through small-group activity that there is a wide spectrum of interest in the Lord's work throughout the whole world can be a healthy corrective.

Furlough Missionary Involvement

An important corollary of this is that missionaries who have been sent out by local churches should not spend their whole furlough engaged in the rat race known as "deputation," apparently planned so as to fit it the maximum number of meetings rather than with a considered strategy for arousing involvement and interest. Far too many missionaries still spend the time they have in their homeland hurtling from one meeting to another, repeating again and again the same two or three stereotyped messages until their presentation becomes stale both to themselves and to their hearers. When Paul and Barnabas returned from their first term of service in Cyprus and Galatia to the congregation from which "they had been commended to the grace of God for the work that they had fulfilled," they not only gathered the church together and "declared all that God had done with them, and how he had opened a door of faith to the Gentiles," but they also "remained no little time with the disciples" (Acts 14:26ff.).

How wonderful it is when modern missionaries on furlough are permitted by their missions to do just that. Would that more sending churches would insist that "their missionaries" should spend a considerable portion of their furlough with their home congregation. A certain amount of "deputation" elsewhere is desirable so that other congregations may hear of missionary work in which their own congregation's missionaries may not be involved. But it seems highly desirable that the definite relationship with a particular congregation should be fostered and encouraged by spending a considerable time with them. The missionary needs the opportunity of becoming once again thoroughly involved in the "body-life" of the congregation. Instead of being the missionary from Bongo-Jumboland who spoke at the evening service for forty minutes, he becomes known on Christian name terms to many in the congregation and the mutual inter-relation of the members find fresh expression. The missionaries have the opportunity to be of blessing in the congregation through personal contact, testimony, and teaching. They may be used by the Lord as soul winners to add new members. They may give spiritual counsel and encouragement to others.

The relationship is anything but one-sided. The missionaries themselves will be heartened, encouraged, and counseled by their fellow Christians, and their relationship together will once again be deepened and cemented. The problem of leaving secondary-school-age children at home can be considerably alleviated when a congregation feels responsible and welcomes the children into the homes of the community. There is also a clear application as far as the care of retired workers is concerned.

Conclusion

It will be seen from this that a new look at the doctrine of the church has exciting implications for whole areas of church life which have become stereotyped and traditional. We suddenly see what missionary work is all about. It arises perfectly logically from our worldwide concern for the growth and perfection of the universal church of Jesus Christ. Our increasing involvement and dedication to the perfection of our own local congregation inevitably deepens our enthusiasm for doing the same thing the world over. Our experience and training in the local situation also whets our appetite and fits us for the possibility of serving overseas. Those trained as dedicated workers in our local church are qualified and able to respond to the congregation when it wishes to send them out as missionaries. In the New Testament it is those who are already active, involved members of the congregation who are selected by them to go elsewhere. Silas was a leading man among the brethren in Jerusalem, and Barnabas, as we saw earlier, was a man whose gifts had already been tremendously appreciated in that same congregation. Even Timothy, young as he was, was appreciated not only by his home congregation in Lystra, but was apparently well-spoken of by those in the nearby church in Iconium as well (Acts 16:2).

A proper biblical view of the church helps us to have a proper biblical view of missions. If our view of the church at home is inadequate, then it is scarcely surprising that we cannot comprehend what mission is all about. On the other hand, if we have a dynamic view of the church as a whole, then it follows almost automatically that we shall have a healthy and proper understanding of missionary work. We shall desire to be as deeply involved in it as we possibly can. And who would want to stop us?

Chapter 10—The Church Militant

But thanks be to God, who in Christ always leads us in triumphal procession, and through us spreads the fragrance of the knowledge of him everywhere (2 Cor 2:14).

Although we are part of a generation which rightly abominates the militaristic nationalism of the past, we cannot reject the metaphor of the church militant without neglecting a very substantial strand of biblical teaching. In the Old Testament, many of the outstanding men of God expressed their leadership and their faith, and experienced the help of God, in military terms.[1] The people of God needed to defend themselves from a whole succession of military invaders—Philistines, Midianites, Egyptians, the dreaded Assyrians, and the Babylonians. The New Testament uses the military metaphor so frequently that to ignore it would give a distorted picture of the church regarded as a corporate body. We must not overlook the fact that the church anticipates opposition and resistance to its victorious advance. The corporate Christian life is seen frequently as a battle and a warfare, and never as a picnic!

The Problem of Achieving the New Community

I hope that this book has stirred us up to a fresh vision of what the new community ought to be as God's beautiful people. But an idealistic dream of what the *ekklésia* ought to be is not enough. We want to see the new community beginning to be realized. The practical ones among us

---

[1] This, however, never meant that the Lord was regarded as a tribal god of battle. For the Lord of hosts was Lord of the heavenly hosts, not, in a military sense, of Israel's armies. The latter were frequently defeated as a result of their own disobedience and idolatry when the Lord used other nation's armies as his agents of judgment.

will have seen the problems already and the less practical among us will experience them soon enough.

Sadly, as we have seen, many in the churches do not want anything more demanding than Sunday attendance. All of us tend to shrink from deeper involvement and may even be afraid of a corporate life where we are not able to hide our inconsistencies. Such barriers are not going to be broken down easily; there is bound to be struggle and conflict. It is not enough merely to *talk* about the new community. But in seeking to make it a reality, some of us will become discouraged and disenchanted with the congregations to which we belong—not just with other people but with ourselves as well. We shall despair of ever climbing out of our ruts of formalism. We have fled from genuine encounter and communication into clichés and stereotyped meetings. We shall be discouraged at how little we are able at first to achieve.

We marvel at these men who "looked forward to the city" and who lived in "deserts and mountains, and in dens and caves of the earth" (Heb 11:10, 38) without attaining what was promised. Even our Lord Jesus himself, coming to save his people from their sins and to inaugurate the new community, could so easily have become discouraged by the twelve, who were anything but a perfect community in embryo. He had to endure not only the cross and the hostility of sinners against himself (Heb 12:2, 3) but also the depressing failures of his followers. They quarreled with one another, argued who would be the greatest, repeatedly evidenced the smallness of their faith, failed to understand the goal of his ministry, and finally forsook him and fled.

You may wonder what the military analogy has to do with all this. We must all have come across the type of achievement story that begins with a group of raw and unpromising recruits from unhopeful backgrounds who are shown being hammered into shape on the barrack square by the tough (but golden-hearted!) sergeant. Then in the stress of battle they learn to appreciate one another, to sacrifice for each other, and are knit together into an effective fighting force. A group of improbable people from a variety of impossible backgrounds become a community! That is the basic plot, and it has certainly happened repeatedly in real life.

Now you may think that there is nothing like that in your Bible. But a closer look reveals (what the AV tends to obscure) that it's there in one of the New Testament Letters: "rejoicing to see your ordered ranks and solid phalanx."[2] Here is the technical language of the Roman barrack square (and suddenly we remember Paul's acquaintance with the praetorian guard; see Phil 1:13), applied as a compliment to the Colossian congregation. Such a disciplined array and close phalanx does not come without drill and effort and hours of miserable "square-bashing" to achieve that consciousness of team work and harmony of movement which is the drill sergeant's goal for his men. Neither may we expect that the harmonious working together as a local "body of Christ" will be achieved without a measure of discipline and painful effort, for we are looking not merely for an integration of bodily movement, but of creative thinking, spiritual gifts and complementary character.

Gideon's 300 men were selected not so much for their military prowess as for their drinking habits, though they did not have a hand free for using a sword anyway. They needed a measure of synchronization, however, in the shouting, trumpet-blowing, pitcher-breaking, and torch-waving which they would be expected to carry out. We remember David's mighty men, so wonderfully described as "mighty and experienced warriors, expert with shield and spear, whose faces were like the faces of lions and who were swift as gazelles upon the mountains" (1 Chr 12:8). This, surely, is something which should be applied to the spiritual valor and training of an ordinary Christian congregation in becoming a fighting community.

We may be tempted to despair of our congregation and wonder if these dry bones can live. So Ezekiel, in the forced-labor camp by the irrigation canal Chebar in the flat plain of Mesopotamia, must have wondered, when he saw the sorry remnant of God's people scattered in exile. When, in his famous vision, responding to the Lord's command, he prophesied to the dry bones, they first came together into proper articulation (*katartismos*!), and then the breath came into them and they stood up, "an exceedingly great army" (Ezek 37:10b). He is a God who makes us alive together (Eph 2:5b), and so he promises that he will "raise you from your graves, O my people. And I will put my Spirit within you, and you shall live" (Ezek 37:13b-14a). The dry bones of the institutionalized churches may be made to live if we preach to them the living Word of God about the people of God, and if the Holy Spirit makes this new community alive together.

---

[2] Colossians 2:5, Greek. See J. B. Lightfoot, *St Paul's Epistles to the Colossians and to Philemon* (Basingstoke, United Kingdom: Macmillan Publishers, 1875), *ad loc*.

The War on the Saints

The New Testament abounds with military images and allusions. Satan makes "war on the saints" (Rev 13:7a), and we "do not wrestle against flesh and blood, but against the rulers, against the authorities, against the cosmic powers over this present darkness, against the spiritual forces of evil in the heavenly places" (Eph 6:12).

This is a dimension which is brought out most clearly by the military metaphor, and which otherwise we might overlook. It is not only that we are trying to perfect ourselves as a morally beautiful community, a new society, but that we are engaged in a spiritual conflict against external evil forces who are doing their utmost to hinder and to spoil the church by various means. Nehemiah succeeded in rebuilding the walls of Jerusalem but had to face much opposition from people who tried to stop him doing it. Where the church is small and weak, the spiritual foe tries direct intimidation and indirect propaganda warfare. He ridicules the church and our pathetic efforts to establish a new community. Where the church is large, but not particularly effective, he will try infiltration to establish a "fifth column." Our Lord's picture is of the enemy sowing tares among the wheat. We must never forget that there are devilish forces doing their utmost to spoil the church of God. It is true that "the gates of hell" will not prevail against it, but they will certainly try to do so. Frequently our trouble is that we have forgotten this biblical truth. We see our problem in largely organizational or methodological terms. If only we start this meeting or follow this method, we are told, we shall see our congregations transformed. We so easily forget that there are spiritual forces opposed to the church and doing their utmost to destroy it. We need to catch the atmosphere of C. S. Lewis' novels, or even his children's books, where this sense of the spiritual enemies of God's people is so strong. The church is not quite as nice and respectable and middle-class as we may imagine. Our venerable European church buildings with their attractive flowers and stained-glass windows mislead us, maybe. We dislike the military flags that would endeavor to identify God with our national interests, and we regard the knight in armor lying peacefully upon his coffin lid as an interesting historical relic. But once, people took refuge in church buildings and rang the bells to warn of marauding pirates. Some buildings to this day carry marks of cannonballs and musket shot. Perhaps they will remind us of the constant spiritual warfare against the church. Just because Sir Arthur Sullivan wrote the music of "Onward, Christian

Soldiers,"[3] we should not imagine that there is anything very Gilbert and Sullivan about the warfare. Church history with its persecutions, apostasy, and schisms is surely sufficient evidence of the spiritual forces of evil attacking the church.

From the very outset Satan was attacking the leaders of the infant church that he might sift them like wheat (Luke 22;31). Alarmed at the genuine dedication of those giving sacrificially to the church, Satan fills the heart of Ananias and Sapphira to counterfeit this spirituality (Acts 5:3). Writing to the church at Rome about those who "cause divisions and create obstacles contrary to the doctrine that you have been taught" (Rom 16:17b), Paul sees behind them the subtle machinations of the enemy but assures them that "the God of peace will soon crush Satan under your feet" (Rom 16:20a). He reminds the Corinthians that we must take care "that we would not be outwitted by Satan; for we are not ignorant of his designs" (2 Cor 2:11). The apostle Peter warns the churches, "Be sober-minded; be watchful. Your adversary the devil prowls around like a roaring lion, seeking someone to devour" (1 Pet 5:8). Peter sees the devil as the adversary of the flock of God, ever prowling round, looking for stragglers. The apostle John, prophesying "in the Spirit" to the seven churches of Asia Minor, repeatedly sees the dangerous influence of Satan in the background of the churches' flirtation with false teaching, and warns, "Behold, the devil is about to throw some of you into prison, that you may be tested, and for ten days you will have tribulation. Be faithful unto death, and I will give you the crown of life" (Rev 2:10b).

These verses are sufficient, surely, to indicate that the spiritual battle is not just a metaphor. Sometimes, I think we are too prone to react against those whom we regard as having an obsession about the work of the devil, people who see theological wolves lurking behind every green tree to snap up the spiritual Red Riding Hood. The fact remains that there is ample biblical evidence which speaks of a spiritual war against the church. And the attack is all the more difficult to combat because of its very subtlety as a war of subversion.

A Corporate Battle

Certainly, the individual Christian is to "wage the good warfare" (1 Tim 1:18b) and to fight a "good fight" (2 Tim 4:7a). There will be constant individual skirmishes and fierce single combat, especially if we are ever

---

[3] Arthur S. Sullivan and Sabine Baring-Gould, 1871.

cut off from the main body. But the major engagements are to be fought by the ordered ranks and close of phalanx of the congregation as a whole. We have already reminded ourselves that the famous picture of the warriors' armor is a plural rather than an individualistic concept.[4] Doubtless Paul thought about armor because his daily contact with Roman guards, to whom he was chained in the prison, made him familiar with the creaking of the soldier's accoutrements. The various items of equipment, however, are nearly all mentioned in the Old Testament as the armor of the Messiah (e.g. Isa 11:5; 52:7; 59:17). It is not only that the armor is provided by God, it is the Lord's own armor, in which he has already been victorious, with which the Christian congregation is to gird itself. A corporate exposition of the armor is in order because it is the whole congregation in Ephesus (or whatever other congregation is reading the Letter) who are engaged in wrestling and fighting against the spiritual forces of wickedness.

1. *The belt of truth*

    The source reference (Isa 11:5) suggests that this does not refer to *doctrinal* truth as such, but rather to sincerity and genuineness. Paul had spoken of this earlier: "Therefore, having put away falsehood (pseudos), let each one of you speak the truth with his neighbor, for we are members one of another" (Eph 4:25). The corporate reference here is clear; truth and integrity are essential because we now belong to each other in the one body. Phillips translates it delightfully, "For we are not separate units." Instead of hiding behind a false mask of assumed piety, there must be a readiness to reveal ourselves and our problems as they really are, so that we can help one another. At first sight a belt is not an item of armor as such at all, until one remembers that formerly prisoners had their belts and their boots removed, as it is difficult to run away very fast in bare feet while holding up one's trousers! Paul writes to Timothy about a "good conscience" (1 Tim 1:19a) and David prays for "truth in the inward being" (Psa 51:6). A belt is basic to armor because it holds everything else in place.

    I still remember a Japanese man who joined himself to our little congregation. He brought people to meetings, spoke in the open air, and offered for house meetings the room he shared with his sister. There was a nagging doubt in some of our minds about him, which suddenly came sharply into focus when we discovered

---

4   See chapter 2: "Salvation More Than Personal," under the heading "Confusions of English Grammar."

that the girl was not his sister. Thereafter we did not know what we could believe. Did he come from where he said? Had he been converted when he said? Once having forfeited his credibility, and lost his girdle of integrity, we did not know how much of what he said was true.

It is essential that there be mutual trust and love in the fighting units of the congregation, and that we should be able to rely utterly upon one another's integrity. It is not surprising, therefore, that Paul puts this first of all in the list of the armor. There has to be, with all our failings, weaknesses and inconsistencies, that true heart-desire to live for the Lord. It is this sincerity of conscience and open integrity that makes true fellowship possible.

2. *The breastplate of righteousness*
The Old Testament word means a coat of mail (Isa 59:17), and the New Testament word (*thōrax*) also means a corselet, which protects both front and back. Is this the righteousness which is *imputed* to us through Christ's death by justification, or is this a righteousness of sanctification actually *imparted* to us? I think both; for both alike are from God; both alike result from Christ's atoning work ministered to us through his Holy Spirit. The essential evidence of belonging to Christ[5] is a changed life, first of the individual, then of his family, and then of the whole new community. Living with known inconsistencies of which we have not repented is to give the devil a loophole (Eph 4:27) and is like going into battle with great holes in one's chain mail. Our sins are not just our personal and private business; the whole group is affected by our failure. A unit of the Roman army of which half the men had left their breastplates behind would be exceedingly vulnerable. Is it not true that we feel sick and hurt when someone known to us in the congregation falls into open sin? Our own faith is undermined and our morale is impaired through the moral inconsistencies of others. Whether we like it or not, others are affected for good or ill by the way we live. The whole testimony of the Christian group can be hindered through sin which has not been dealt with. Thus, the transformed and beautiful life of the congregation is essential to its effectiveness in battle.

---

[5] Publishers note: That is, in sanctification.

3. *Shoes ready with the gospel of peace*

Isaiah suggests that the soldiers were also messengers bringing peace (Isa 52:7). The "liberation" brought by many armies is certainly a mockery. How true it is that, wherever Christ's messengers go, they should bring Christ's peace with them. God's people, as we have seen, are on the march; and it is the extreme mobility of the Roman army moving at high speed along its well-made military roads that gives us this picture of the soldiers' sandals. We are in territory which has been occupied by forces hostile to our King, and wherever we go together we seek to bring his liberating peace.

4. *The shield of faith*

The Greek word has affinity with the word for a door. The shields were large and oblong and afforded good protection to the individual. But when the hostile tribes of wild Welsh or Picts appeared, the Roman column would turn towards them and the front rank would kneel, their shields placed edge to edge. The second rank would take a pace forward, so that their shields formed a second tier—a double row of shields making a solid wall, while the third rank would hurl javelins and other missiles over the top at the unfortunate enemy. An individual on his own would be rapidly encircled. But in the group, the soldiers' shields made a solid wall of defense.

We *need* other Christians in our fight against spiritual wickedness and the attacks of Satan. So often, we struggle along as individuals in our lonely battles, and fail to avail ourselves of the protection of the caring group, praying defensively for one another in the congregation where individuals can share their problems with others. The shield of faith is effective when it is used in conjunction with the faith of others. Our fellowship in the congregation needs to afford that kind of mutual protection.

5. *The helmet of salvation*

A parallel passage (Paul enjoyed this armor theme and used it also in Rom 13:12-14 and 1 Thess 5:5-8) suggests that this is the "hope of salvation" (1 Thess 5:8); that is, the certainty of final salvation ? and ultimate victory. The helmet was essential to confidence in battle: it enabled you to see your enemies and aim blows at them. Without it you were always ducking and hiding behind your shield, and therefore somewhat vulnerable. It is essential that we

Christians be certain that final victory is ours, and that the day is coming when every knee will bow and every tongue confess that Jesus is Lord. Pessimistic Christians who walk around glumly talking about the ruin of the church and the post-Christian era, thus spreading defeatism and gloom in the ranks, are like men without their helmets, weakening the whole unit. We need to have that absolute assurance that the gates of hell will not prevail against the church and that the "full number of the Gentiles" will come in.

I still remember being summoned as a boy together with the rest of the school to be addressed by General Bernard Montgomery, as he was then. "Monty" had been inspecting troops in our school grounds in preparation for the D Day invasion of Europe, and decided that he would like to speak to the boys. There he was, this famous figure with his beret and rows of medal ribbons. His theme was "Know your enemy." The message that came through loud and clear was: "The German soldier is the finest fighting man the world has ever seen, and—it takes someone like me to beat him!" I remember afterwards discussing this with a group of other boys. "Did you ever hear anyone quite so cocksure and swollen-headed? The possibility of defeat doesn't seem even to have entered his head!" And that, as someone observed, was probably why he was a victorious general. He was wearing the helmet of "salvation," if you like.

Defeat did not enter his head.

We also need that same utter confidence in Christ's ultimate victory, as well as in his power to win battles along the way. It is not, of course, confidence in our own power, but a confidence in the power of God. As Christians we need to share this spiritual optimism and to be ever looking for opportunities to experience the victory of Christ. Whether one thinks of missionaries or of congregations, morale, in my experience, is of crucial importance. The defeatist attitude of cynics and pessimists can be grievously infectious. The enemy's propaganda warfare is aimed to persuade us that we can never win. He makes us afraid of a fictional, irresistible temptation to shake our assurance. It is the certainty of the victory of Christ that is the helmet of salvation, which all the congregation must wear for battle.

6. *The sword of the Spirit* Christ himself used the Word of God against the temptations of Satan, repeatedly reminding himself, "It is written…" (Matt 4:4, 7, 10), quoting passages which speak of the dependence of man upon God for supplying his needs, of the fact that man must not put God to the test, and that he must worship only the Lord.

We likewise need to use the Word of God as a defensive weapon against temptation, hiding his Word in our hearts so that we do not sin against him (Psa 119:11). We also use the sword of the Spirit as an offensive weapon, so that others may be liberated from the power of the enemy. Here again we so frequently think of the individual using his Bible in this way. But surely, in this corporate context, we cannot continue to think individualistically, but must rather echo those stirring words of the Psalmist: "Let the high praises of God be in their throats, and two-edged swords in their hands" (Psa 149:6).

When we make the Word of God our guide in the congregation, and study it together in our small groups, 'drilling together' as it were, we are all helped and encouraged and taught. This corporate use of Scripture is found not only of the noble Jews in the synagogue at Berea, where "they received the word with all eagerness, examining the Scriptures daily to see if these things were so" (Acts 17:11b), but also very wonderfully of the Christians in the church at Rome:

> For whatever was written in former days was written for our instruction, that through endurance and through the encouragement of the Scriptures we might have hope. May the God of endurance and encouragement grant you to live in such harmony with one another, in accord with Christ Jesus, that together you may with one voice glorify the God and Father of our Lord Jesus Christ. Therefore welcome one another as Christ has welcomed you, for the glory of God. (Rom 15:4-6)

It is the corporate use of the Scriptures that brings the Roman believers into harmony with each other and leads them out into acceptable praise.

7. *The warriors' attitude of prayer* The Holy Spirit gives to us, as God's people, "access in one Spirit to the Father" (Eph 2:18), and we are to make use of this privilege by praying at all times in (or by)

the Spirit. There need be no special "charismatic" meaning here, but a simple reminder to use the means which God has provided through his Holy Spirit. The Spirit has provided the Word of God; therefore, "Take the sword of the Spirit," and make use of it. The Spirit provides the medium of immediate access to the presence of God; therefore take your privilege and use it. The chief sin of Christians is neglect. It is not that we need some new, hitherto unrevealed, secret blessing, but that we have been neglecting secrets to which we have long given lip-service and intellectual assent, but which we have not experienced and enjoyed. It is not that God does not provide all that we need to perfect the new community (see 2 Pet 1:3), but that we have neglected the means which God has graciously provided.

It is not that God does not answer prayer, but that we neglect to pray.

God has already provided all the means of grace, but we neglect to appropriate them, and thus we experience poverty and want, both as individuals and even more as congregations. How few congregations there are that really pray! We all agree *in theory* that we ought, but *in practice* we neglect to do so. Again and again, one meets congregations where distress is expressed at the lack of conversions and frustration at the lack of joy in congregational life. "Where is the 'body-life' that there ought to be?," they ask.

When you start asking questions, you discover that there is little or no corporate prayer. There may be an occasional prayer meeting, but either very few attend it, or it is mainly given over to preaching; and there is still very little corporate congregational prayer. We may be despairing about seeing the body-life of the new community; perhaps it is because we do not want it enough to be praying about it. A congregation needs to be so dissatisfied with its spiritual dryness, and so long to see a change, and to become a real community enjoying an extended family life, that it begins to call upon the Lord to work in them to will and to work for his good pleasure (*i.e.* what he delights to do).

The idea that we should be on the alert (*cf.* Mark 14:38) suggests that we should have a mutual, prayerful concern so that we are on watch to defend one another from surprise attack. We need to have our sentries out, so that none is caught and taken captive because of lack of vigilance. Thus, this whole passage in Ephesians about the Christian battle, and many other passages of the New Testament as well, are full of rich, corporate teaching when we consider them in a congregational sense.

The Battlefield of the World

What is the relationship between the church and the world? We do not fight against flesh and blood, and yet we are reminded by Christ himself that the world around us is hostile to the new kingdom.

> "If the world hates you, know that it has hated me before it hated you. If you were of the world, the world would love you as its own; but because you are not of the world, but I chose you out of the world, therefore the world hates you" (John 15:18, 19).

Let there be no confusion here. As Christians we are concerned about a new society. But this is not an earthly Utopia, it is the church of God. We are to redeem a new community out of the old world, but we cannot redeem the hostile world system organized in opposition against God. We must never forget the clear opposition of the two groups in Christ's teaching. We see it so clearly in his parables of the sheep and the goats, and the wheat and the tares. We want to build a new society, but it is a new society within the old. We have to go into the world to make disciples from all nations. We have to be the light of the world so that it is not entirely swallowed up by darkness. We have to be the salt of the earth so that our human systems are preserved from complete corruption. As Kraemer puts it, "The church is antithetical to the world, and yet bound to it by infinite commitment."[6] Here, then, is the paradox that Christians are in the world and yet not of it. Kraemer goes on to speak of the "dispersion of the church through the laity in the world." But let us be in no doubt whatever that we are nonetheless under attack, and there is constant pressure either in direct, rationalistic attacks upon all religions, or through the more subtle inroads of a humanistic persuasion to throw away our arms and surrender to the enemy.

Jerusalem must not be confused with Babylon.

The new city is the exact counterpart of what man had wanted to do—not in the sense of obverse and reverse, or type and antitype, but rather in the sense of the back of a woven rug and its right side. While the side man

---

[6] Kraemer, *A Theology of the Laity*, p. 182.

works on is a formless mess, the side God works on is the right side, the side of the New Jerusalem. God's presence is the essential point in whatever may be said about the city. He is taking possession of the world from which man wanted Him excluded.[7]

And this is the thrilling and the wonderful thing. God is developing the "one new man," or better, the "one new humanity." It is as though the church, the people of God, is a new race of individuals, a new species, mutants, *homo Christoferens* suddenly appearing among the old *homo sapiens*. The new creation has resulted in a new race of Christian men forming themselves into the new community.

Os Guinness, concluding his book *The Dust of Death*, reminds us that the early Christians were commonly called "the third race," (*genus tertius*; there were Greeks, Jews, and Christians).

> They were a healing community, they were one in Christ, they were a Third Race. All classification by nation, race, ideology, religion or class structure denoted a previous reality now transcended by Christian truth.[8]

What is the Attitude of the New Community to the Old Society?

The world in which we live falls into natural groupings. We feel less affinity with those outside our own family, yet we still have some kinship with those from the same home town, or from our own nation when overseas, or with our own race. This is recognized in Scripture.

> And he made from one man every nation of mankind to live on all the face of the earth, having determined allotted periods and the boundaries of their dwelling place (Acts 17:26).

But Christians in the third race were not restricted in their obligations merely to their "in group." They felt an obligation "both the Greeks and to barbarians" (Rom 1:14). The whole "good Samaritan" ethic and concern to love one's neighbor is something quite foreign to Confucian-Buddhist thinking. The Confucian is caught in a web of complex obligations but is not eager to take on any more. In Japan, the man injured by the roadside will attract spectators, but probably little active help, until the police or ambulance comes. To be aggressively helpful suggests you

---

[7] Jacques Ellul, *The Meaning of the City* (Grand Rapids, MI: Eerdmans Publishing Co., 1970), p. 190.

[8] Os Guinness, *The Dust of Death* (Westmont, IL: InterVarsity Press, 1973), p. 368.

feel responsible, so that you are immediately a police suspect. Why else would you help someone you do not know?

If suffering is an illusion, then why give help which may be unwelcome anyway, for the person helped will then feel under obligation?

The Christian, on the other hand, sees himself as a debtor to all. To him suffering is real, and neighbors are to be loved. The Christian is not an isolated, existential, unrelated observer, but he must be deeply involved with his neighbor and his need. The Bible commands a separation from worldliness, but not from needy men and women in the world (1 Cor 5:9, 10).

- 500 households needing a neighborly hand of friendship
- 100 elderly, housebound people, living alone
- 100 deprived children
- 100 broken marriages
- 100 juvenile delinquents who have been before the courts in the last three years
- 20 unmarried mothers
- 10 discharged prisoners
- 10 homeless
- 20 families in debt trouble
- 80 persons in hospital
- 80 alcoholics

Many Christians are ignorant of the degree of need. Some statistics from the city of Birmingham[9] indicate that around the average evangelical church there are 2,000 houses, with 10,000 people who could walk to the church within ten or fifteen minutes. You can reckon that there are:

> So then, as we have opportunity, let us do good to everyone, and especially to those who are of the household of faith. (Gal 6:10).

It is not that the new community is unaware of belonging to an "in group" for there are those who are "outsiders" (Col 4:5). But the body of Christ is not a closed, selfish society concerned only with its own self-interest like a trade union, or a friendly society, or other forms of social insurance and mutual protection. The new community is open-ended and always ready, not only to serve people with a view to bringing them to faith, but to serve their neighbors altruistically, because this is what

---

[9] Supplied by the Project Group from Phaesey Evangelical Church in an article in *Echoes of Service* (February, 1974).

God, who sends his sun to shine on both the just and the unjust, is like (Matt 5:45b).

This is his will for his people.

The Christian, then, is prepared to be friendly and to expect friendliness in return—or even hostility, for he knows that Christ's liberating army is in territory which has been subject to and may still be sympathetic to the enemy, and among them are agents of the enemy biding their time. But he longs to win them over.

The new community will see itself as the third race, a new and distinct entity, quite distinct from the old society around it. We must not ignore the world and run away from it; we must endeavor to work and to witness within it. But we must not confuse it with the church.

> The Christian should participate in social and political efforts in order to have an influence in the work, not with the hope of making a paradise, but simply to make it more tolerable. Not to diminish the opposition between this world and the Kingdom of God, but simply to modify the opposition between the disorder of this world and the order of preservation that God wants it to have. Not to bring in the Kingdom of God, but so that the Gospel might be proclaimed in order that all men might truly hear the good news.[10]

Enthusiastic contemporary Christians sometimes talk as though the church's only hope for survival is to adapt itself like a kind of corporate chameleon, a federal Vicar of Bray! Certainly, we live in changing days. Aquila and Priscilla used the same building as home, workshop, and church meeting place. Today, Mr. Aquila would doubtless commute to the tentmaking factory on the other side of the megalopolis and probably commute also to attend a congregation.

"Change is the essence of life. The moment we cease to change, to be able to adapt, to adjust, to respond effectively to new situation, then we have begun to die."[11] Christians have always been concerned to adapt themselves to different societies, as Paul did to the differing contemporaneous sub-cultures of Jews and Greeks (1 Cor 9:19-23). We must not be like ostriches with our heads in the sand. But neither must we pursue novelty and become contemporary chameleons for fear that otherwise we may be left an ecclesiastical dinosaur upon the sands of history!

---

[10] Jacques Ellul, quoted by Carl Henry in *Aspects of Social Ethics* (Grand Rapids, MI: Eerdmans Publishing Co., 1964), p. 96.

[11] Lee Kwan Yew, Prime Minister of Singapore, quoted in *The Mirror* (8 May, 1967).

Rather let the church show itself to be the church, the third race and new community, changing from one degree of beauty to another.

The Certainty of Final Triumph

We have already referred to the triumph procession to indicate that the concept of a 'love demo' is not so far-fetched as it might at first seem. Roman generals came back victorious with their plunder and their prisoners. Anyone who has smelled an Asian army on the march after a few hours in tropical heat will understand why it was customary to burn spices along the line of march like a kind of imperial Airwick! This Paul likens to our bearing the fragrance of Christ with us wherever we go (2 Cor 2:14ff.). In the procession also were the earthenware vessels, unadorned and utilitarian in themselves but containing talents of gold and silver. This Paul makes a picture of the unimpressive and insignificant Christian, carrying in his frail, mortal body the treasure of the gospel, the very life of God (2 Cor 4:7). In the procession are those who are led in triumph, those taken captive by the victorious king and given to his people to serve them as slaves (Eph 4:1, 8, 11), among whose number Paul the apostle sees himself, taken prisoner on the road to Damascus. But most significant of all is the victorious general. A greater than Caesar is here, Lord of lords and King of kings. His triumph is inevitable. Already, on the cross, he has "disarmed the rulers and authorities and put them to open shame, by triumphing over them in him" (Col 2:15).

Paul the missionary, afflicted, perplexed, persecuted, struck down (2 Cor 4:8), is quite undaunted by his trials and sufferings. The victorious counter culture is on the march. Roszak describes the primitive Christian community as "absolute nobodies, the very scum of the earth".[12]

Brunner is clear about the conflict which may ensue:

> With or without the churches, if necessary even in opposition to them, God will cause the *ecclesia* to become a real community of brothers.

---

[12] Roszak, *The Making of a Counter Culture.*, p. 43.

Or again he says:

> Not the hostility of the unbelieving world, but clerical par-
> sonic ecclesiasticism has ever been the greatest enemy of the
> Christian message and of brotherhood rooted in Christ.[13]

These words may seem harsh when one remembers faithful, godly pastor-teachers the world over struggling on inadequate stipends to build
the church. But it is the hardened system rather than the men that have
aroused Brunner's wrath. And who among us has not felt frustration
with the structures of ecclesiastical and ecumenical organization? It is
possible that that system may try to hold back the tide of reform, and
be left behind by it. But no-one who knows of the wedding of the bride
wants to be like an unprepared foolish bridesmaid without oil to keep
her lamp burning.

> Surely it is time for us to meet one another in penitent
> acknowledgement of our common failure to be what the
> church ought to be.[14]

Where do we ourselves stand? Are we in that triumphal procession or
standing in its way? Christ's challenge is abundantly clear: "Whoever
is not with me is against me, and whoever does not gather with me
scatters" (Matt 12:30). And as we agonize and wonder how we can turn
congregations into fighting units in his triumph, and wonder if we can
ever overcome all the obstacles in the way, his voice comes with calm
assurance, "I will build my church" (Matt 16:18b).

The Call to Arms

When Saul was first made king, there went with him "men of valor
whose hearts God had touched" (1 Sam 10:26b). When news came of
what Nahash was doing to some of the people of God, the Holy Spirit
came mightily upon Saul and, as a result of the summons he sent, "they
came out as one man" (1 Sam 11:6, 7). They responded to a call to arms;
as, earlier, the tribes had responded to Gideon when the Holy Spirit took
possession of him and he sounded the trumpet (Judg 6:34).

---

[13] Brunner, *The Misunderstanding of the Church*, pp. 118, 117. It should be noted that Brunner
is not against decency and order. For example, he writes, "When Paul is enumerating the
various charismata to which the special types of service are adapted, he includes the charisma of
kybernēsis, or government, as one amongst others without according to it the slightest degree of
preference. This service too is needed, so he argues, and the charisma corresponding to it exists;
but this service is only one among others and authorises no sort of hierarchical structure."

[14] Newbigin, *The Household of God*, p. 134.

Albert Camus is reported as saying,

> The world expects of Christians that they will raise their voices so loudly and clearly, and so formulate their protest, that not even the simplest man can have the slightest doubt about what they are saying. Further, the world expects of Christians that they will eschew all fuzzy abstractions and plant themselves squarely in front of the bloody face of history. We stand in need of folk who have determined to speak directly and unmistakably and come what may, to stand by what they have said.[15]

How are we going to respond to this book about the church? How can we be hearers as well as doers of this word?

For all of us it means a determination to take the congregation seriously, and not as a rather ineffective means of grace. It means getting as involved as we can possibly be in seeking to make the church into an extended family, a warm living community. It means that we shall all seek to exercise our spiritual gifts in a congregational setting, to realize the body-life of the congregation in our gatherings, so that the body is edified and grows together in love.

For some of us it may mean responding to the call of the congregation to become a pastor-teacher, or an evangelist, or a missionary (I could never leave that out!), because this building of the church matters so much that it matters more than anything else, and I will train and prepare and study for the kind of ministry that the Bible shows to be required. It is not that I want to lord it over my brethren in a petty local dictatorship, in a one-man band type of ministry, but rather that I long to "equip the saints for the work of ministry, for building up the body of Christ" (Eph 4:12).

This is something worth dedicating our lives to—all of us—God's beautiful people.

Better start praying, then, about how to realize it.

---

15 In John H. Court, *The Function of the Christian within the Realm of the Ongoing Power Struggle* (Flinders University, South Australia, 1973). p. 103.

Scripture Index

Genesis
3:9 4

Exodus
6:7 20
19:5-6 19

Deuteronomy
4:10 3
7:6 . . . . .5, 19
9:10 3
14:26 105
18:16 3
31:30 3

Judges
6:34 141
20:2 3

First Samuel
3:4 4
4:21 93
10:26 141
11:6-7 141

Second Samuel
7:27 30

First Chronicles
12:8 127

Psalms
22:22 3
51:6 130
119:11 134
149:6 134

Isaiah
11:5 130
52:7 . . . . .130, 132
59:17 . . . . .130, 131
62:5 52
66:1-2 27

Jeremiah
31:31 19

Ezekiel
16:8 52
37:10 127
37:13-14 127
48:35 24

Hosea
2:16 52
2:19-20 52
2:23 19

Amos
9:11-12 . . . . 18, 27

Matthew
1:21 . . . . 11, 18
4:4 134
4:7 134
4:10 134
4:21 45
5:14 68
5:45 139
12:30 141
16:18 . . . . . .19, 29-30, 141

Matthew (cont.)

18:15 81
18:16 81
18:17 81
18:20 . . . . 81, 99
19:12 70
19:28 41
22:30 71

Mark

14:38 135

Luke

1:17 19
1:68 19
1:77 19
2:10 19
2:31-32 19
10:20 57
22:31 129

John

1:14 35
15:18-19. 136

Acts

2:46 84
4:32-5:11 54
5:3. 129
6:14 27
7:38 3
7:48-50 27
8:36-38 84
11:19 85
11:20-21. 85
13:48 83
13:52 83
14:20 83
14:21 83
14:23 83
14:26 123

15:2 82
15:3 79
15:3-4 82
15:14 18
15:14-18. 18
15:15-18. 27
15:32 117
16:2 124
16:33 84
17:11 134
17:26 137
18:27 57
19:32 3
19:37 1
19:41 3
20:4 82
20:6 82
20:20 84
20:27 84
20:28 . . . . 32, 83
20:29-30. 41
20:31 . . . . 59, 83
20:32 32
27 31

Romans

1:14 137
8:14 13
8:16 13
9:25 19
11:25 31
12:4-5 35
12:4-6 42
13:12-14. 132
14 . . . . 40, 60
15:4-6 134
16:1 57
16:5 6
16:17 129
16:20 129

First Corinthians

1:2 6
1:2-9 56
1:9 4
1:10 39
1:11-13 84
1:13 39
3:9 23
3:10-17 28
3:17 29
5:6-8 55
5:9-10 138
5:12 83
7:7 71-72
7:32-35 70
9:19-23 139
10:16-17 . . . . 35, 102
11:18 84
11:29 35
12 . . . . 13, 43
12:7 42
12:11 43
12:12-27 35
12:13 43
12:15 40
12:21 44
12:23 89
12:24-26 44
12:27 . . . . 35, 102
12:31 13
13:9 60
13:12 60
14 . . . . 43, 101
14:1 . . . . 13, 117
14:24 117
14:29 . . . . . . 14, 46, 117
14:31 101
14:39 117
16:10 57

Second Corinthians

2:11 129
2:14 . . . . 125, 140
3:18 . . . . 26, 100
4:7 140
4:8 140
6:16 . . . . . . 19, 28, 100
8:23 . . . . 57, 82, 117
11:2-4 54
13:5 56
13:9 48
13:11 48

Galatians

2:11 60
3:27-29 84
4:19 92
5:22-23 47
6:1 45
6:10 . . . . 65, 138

Ephesians

1:1 16
1:14 16
1:18 16
1:22 5
1:22-23 . . . . 1, 16
2 24
2:1 16
2:5 . . . . 16, 127
2:12 16
2:15 16
2:18 134
2:19 . . . . 16, 63, 65
2:19-22 28
2:20 42
2:21 16
2:21-22 10
2:22 16
3 16
3:4-6 15-16
3:9-11 15

Ephesians (cont.)

3:10 . . . . .5, 17
3:14-15 76
3:16-19 100
3:18 17
3:21 . . . . .4-5, 17
4. . . . . 47, 58
4:1 . . . . 4, 58, 140
4:3-6. 40
4:7 42
4:8 140
4:11 . . . . . .45, 101, 140
4:11-13 117
4:11-16 45
4:12 . . . 36, 45, 47-48, 142
4:13 . . . . 20, 48, 118
4:14 41
4:15 58
4:16 . . . . 36, 46
4:17 58
4:22 58
4:24 58
4:25 . . . . 17, 58, 130
4:27 131
4:28 58
4:29 58
5. 67
5:4. 58
5:18 67
5:19-21 68
5:21 68
5:21-22 84
5:22-33 . . . . 72, 76
5:23-27 53
5:25 10
5:27 . . . . .8, 51, 92
6. 12
6:4. 89
6:12 . . . . 13, 128

6:18 13
15-16 48

Colossians

1:18 5
1:24 5
1:28 59
2:5. 127
2:15 140
2:16 60
2:19 . . . . 36, 46
2:20 60
3:16 59
4:5. 138
4:10 57
4:14 36
4:15-16 36

First Thessalonians

1:1. 6
5:5-8. 132
5:8. 132

First Timothy

1:18 129
1:19 130
3:2. 83
3:4-5. 76
5:1. 90
5:9. 57
5:11 57
5:19 90
6:12 5

Second Timothy

4:7. 129

Titus

1:5. 83
1:5-9. 83
1:6. 84
2:14 19

Philemon

1:13 127
1:19 32
2. 32
2:1-3. 32
2:12 . . . . 31, 92
3:3. 97
3:14 5
4:21 12

Hebrews

2:5. 23
2:10 . . . . 23, 66
2:11 . . . . 23, 66
2:12 . . . . .3, 23, 66
2:13 . . . . .7, 23, 66
2:17 23
3:1. 5
10:24-25. 99
11:10 . . . . 23, 126
11:16 23
11:38 126
12:2-3. 126
12:23 57
13:14 23
13:17 . . . . . . 57, 83, 90
13:20-21. 49

James

5:16-20 60

First Peter

2:4-5. 27
2:5. 102
2:9. . . . . 19, 102
2:10 19
4:10 42
5:5. 90
5:8. 129

Second Peter

1:3. 135
3:18 54

Jude

3. 60

Revelation

2-3. 92
2:5. 29
2:10 129
3:16 29
13:7. 128
21:2 . . . . 23, 52
21:3 20
21:9 52

About Bold Grace Ministries

Purpose Statement

Bold Grace Ministries exists to: **unite** believers under the banner of God's grace (Eph 4:3-6), **share** the gospel and aid those who will proclaim it faithfully (Rom 10:14-15), **increase** believers' confidence in the power of the indwelling Christ (Gal 2:20), **love** without hypocrisy (Rom 12:9a), **proclaim** the hope of Christ's glorious kingdom (Rom 8:18-21), and **equip** the saints to share Christ's matchless grace and love with others (2 Tim 2:2).

Our Vision

Grace is relevant. By grace God makes Himself available to men, and by grace He meets our deepest needs. Grace unites us, when we are naturally so prone to division. It frees us from pride and the tyranny of sin and effects holiness and humility.

Yet too often grace is missing or downplayed in our message about Christ, our interactions with one another, and our views on the Christian life. By God's grace, and with the help of like-minded brothers and sisters, we hope to reach out to the world with a message of God's free grace, to unite and encourage our brothers and sisters in Christ, and to teach all the ways that His grace is sufficient for us in our pursuit of Christlikeness.

Find more Bold Grace books and learn more about
Bold Grace at www.boldgrace.org.

Made in the USA
Middletown, DE
16 January 2021